Notes of Pr

MW00890299

"Change management remains a challenge for every leader. In this new book, Hilary Potts provides practical advice that leaders can immediately put in action and quickly secure enduring results."

Godefridus Vranken,
CEO of Marden Williamson International AG,
former Board member and Head of Business Development and
Corporate Strategy at JT International Holdings BV

"Having worked and lived in the Greater China region for over 20 years, I've witnessed a tremendous amount of change and seen how the best business executives approach, adapt, and execute during such volatile situations. Hilary Potts has prepared a comprehensive and systematic playbook that every executive can use to think through all the key stages of an important change project and, importantly, avoid the most common pitfalls. Every executive should read this book to learn how to lead change."

Warwick John Fahy, author, *Influence: The Jack Ma Way*

"Everyone knows the executive's hardest job is leading change successfully. Too many executives have failed in this enormous task and have paid the consequences. I have found Hilary Potts' counsel at helping me lead change to be invaluable. She has now captured this wisdom in this book."

Andrew Towle, Director, The ReWall Company

"In *The Truth About Change*, accelerating change starts at the top: leaders should aim for accountability, strategy building, and a culture that embraces employees' engagement in this process. The notion of leading change is flipped on its head in Hilary Potts' concise and compelling book."

Lawrence Siff, President and CEO, Neptune Advisors, LLC

"If you are a change leader, this is a book you must read. Better still – read it before you start rolling out the change process. It will ensure that you don't end up falling in the 70 percent of change initiatives that don't succeed. Drawing from her vast knowledge base and experience of having been an operational executive and change leader, Hilary Potts has seen it all. She offers clear thinking, useful frameworks, and actions to consider and apply in your own setting. A must-read!"

Jasbindar Singh, business psychologist, executive coach, and blogger

---

"A CEO's primary role is to prepare for the future. And that future will inevitably involve change. Hilary Potts in her book *The Truth About Change* has given us valuable insights about understanding, preparing for, and executing change. It is a must-read for CEOs of all levels."

Fred W. Green, Chairman of the Chief Executive Officers Club of Boston

---

"*The Truth About Change* provides important tools with a leader change roadmap. It focuses on the important difference between the manager and leader role and how successful transformations start from the top. Hilary Potts masterfully leads you through the chapters in how to communicate, change behavior, and set realistic performance metrics. It is practical, effective, and immediately actionable."

Rudi Scheiber-Kurtz, Founder and CEO of Next Stage Solutions, Inc., and author of *Stop Compromising*

———————

"Hilary Potts book captures the elusive truth that a successful change strategy must include a people strategy. Recognizing the 'human' side of change, this book takes leaders beyond their processes and plans, and provides them with a valuable roadmap for engaging, communicating and motivating people towards sustainable change."

Lisa Bergeron, Founding Partner & Chief Visionary Officer, AWE

———————

"*The Truth About Change* is the most practical book on change leadership ever written. Others have spent time on model construction or theory – this book is for those who want to read and then get it done. If you are a leader who needs to change your organization, this book will save your career. The organization of *The Truth About Change* is simply brilliant – an efficient laydown for busy managers who want to envision their change strategy from start to finish. Any manager who wants to affect change should stop, read Hilary Potts' book, and then – and only then – proceed. It's a refreshing, pragmatic blueprint for engineering effective change in your organization."

Brigadier General Thomas Kolditz, Director, Doerr Institute for New Leaders, Rice University

THE TRUTH ABOUT CHANGE

A Leader's Guide to Successfully Executing Change Initiatives

Hilary Potts

DISCLAIMER

This book should be used only as a general guide and not as the ultimate
source of the information contained herein. You as the leader will know best
what will work in your particular business situation.

Printed in the United States of America

ISBN-13: 978-1975745196
ISBN-10: 1975745191
LCCN: 2017913428
CreateSpace Independent Publishing Platform, North Charleston, SC

Cover and Interior Design and Illustrations by Lynn Amos
Copyedited by Mark Woodworth

Requests for permission to make copies of any part of this work may be made to:
The HAP Group
info@hapgrp.com

To my late dad, Daniel L. Potts, who showed me that adversity is an opportunity to grow.

Contents

Illustrations

Introduction:
The Truth about Change

I am always doing things I can't do. That is how I get to do them.

—Pablo Picasso

In these transformative times, the status quo can be a death sentence to a business. Business press headlines are full of stories about companies in various stages of change – product launches, acquisitions, mergers, new and improved strategies, cost reductions, process and system enhancements – all in the name of bringing the best products and services to market. Change is constant. Change is essential for any leader looking to advance and deliver top performance. Leaders are under significant pressures to achieve new results. What was achieved last month is long forgotten the next.

This book provides insights from my decades of work as both an operating executive and a change leadership consultant. My days are spent working with leaders implementing a variety of change initiatives. I have personally led and experienced both successful and failed initiatives. I have been honored to work with leaders of global companies and iconic brands, each trying to create a "secret sauce" to bring products and services to market. Through my own experiences and significant strategic engagements, I have learned some consistent truths about change, regardless of the type of company, the industry, or location. I want to share these truths with you.

Truth: A business problem or need presents itself, and you look for the best solution possible. Often, the solution involves change.

Leaders who know how to navigate and lead change have a competitive advantage that enables them to reap the rewards in increased revenue and profits. Unfortunately, most leaders, while constantly initiating change, admit they are not very good at actually leading change. You may hold the leadership position and may try to convince yourself that if you just communicate your strategies, processes, and project plans, you'll get the results you want. It doesn't work that way.

Think about it this way: You are moving your company to a "new normal." Some would say there is no "new normal," simply the next change in the evolution of delivering and growing your business. The point is that leaders must have the confidence and capability to lead themselves and others in these changing times. Change leadership competency is part of being a successful business leader who can deliver results.

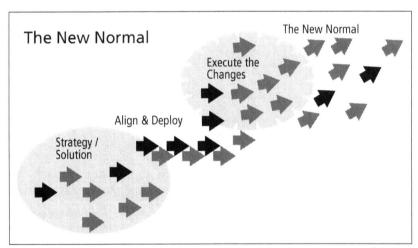

Figure I-1

Truth: If you want a different outcome, you must change what you and your people do. Everyone – from the C-Suite to the person in the field – has a role to play. But often people want the benefits of the change, without being changed. People rarely agree, accept, or adopt a new way merely by being told to "do it."

Truth: Change requires people who are ready, willing, and able to make the change.

If you want the business to achieve its full potential, you need to find ways to engage your people and your organization quickly in working in the new way. You can spend millions on a business solution, but if you can't get people to use the system or deploy the strategy, you will not achieve the results you want.

Truth: Change initiatives are people intensive, and learning a new set of behaviors takes time. You can accelerate the change with the right reinforcement systems and behavioral engagement plans. Regrettably, too many leaders shy away from the human side of change; they find it easier to focus on the business plan tactics.

Truth: Leaders talk about what others need to do differently, but often don't realize that change starts with themselves. It's easy for you to forget you've been working on the strategic initiative for weeks and months, familiarizing yourself with the design and business plan. Once the initiative is announced, you expect people to jump into action. Too frequently, the people don't understand the change or know what they should do. They feel overwhelmed and undersupported; they may do the wrong things, or not act at all.

Why should this matter to you? Your actions can inspire or stall the very outcomes you desire. When people are not fully prepared and engaged, the change initiative falters. Research continues to show that over the last three decades, only 30 percent of change initiatives actually succeeded. Why have they failed? People need a reason to believe in the change. They want to understand what is happening, why it's important, and how it will affect their work.

If they don't believe in the change, they may resist it or fail to consider it worth any effort. While strategies and plans set the course and leaders guide the journey forward, the people are needed to make the change a reality.

Truth: Change is disruptive. It can trigger fear and a multitude of reactions: physical, mental, and emotional. You don't need to be a psychologist, but you do need to find ways to get others engaged in the change; otherwise you may find yourself the only one committed to implementing the change. Leading change requires using both the "hard skills" (business intelligence) and the "soft skills" (emotional and social intelligence) so that you can reap the tangible rewards of your efforts.

Why I Wrote This Book

I have three main reasons for writing this book:

First: Over and over again, I see leaders who think they are accelerating change by not taking the time to work on the people aspects, only to find it is taking longer to implement the solution – or that the goals are missed entirely. Too often, I hear, "We only use change management tools for our larger initiatives." Whether you enlist your change management professionals or go it alone, whenever you are implementing a strategy, project, or initiative that involves people doing something differently, a change-savvy leader knows that the people side of the initiative needs to be addressed. You may not use all the tools in your change toolkit every time, but you use the right tools at the right time to get the most efficient and effective results.

Change leadership is about leaders taking an active role in leading through and with people. Paying attention to the people aspects enables a leader to assess whether people are readily engaging or inadvertently slowing things down due to resistance, confusion, or hesitation to take action. When leaders incorporate the people aspects from the beginning, they can avoid having to make heroic efforts during the implementation to salvage a failing project. I hope that the principles laid out in these pages will enable you and your colleagues to find a simple way to consider the people aspects in your strategic plans.

Second: I want to help leaders like you identify some simple actions you can take to enhance your change effort. Early in my career, I was naïve enough to think that, with the right facts and logic, people would agree on the change and take action; that if you have good enough arguments, people will buy-in. But this is very far from the truth. We need to treat the people-side of leading change with the same focus as we do in crafting strategies and pursuing results.

Third: I want to bridge the gaps between the problem, the solution, and the outcome. There is more to change than the business actions we take. When you understand and pay attention to your people's physical, mental, and emotional reactions, you can guide them to transition from the old way to the new way. How you lead change helps people take the journey with you, instead of digging in their heels and resisting the change.

Overall, this book can help you if:

◆ Your strategies and plans are not yielding the desired results.
◆ It requires heroic efforts to implement changes.
◆ Your brilliant solutions are compromised in implementation.
◆ You and your fellow leaders cannot seem to reach agreement and alignment.
◆ Your team struggles to get people to accept change and take action.

Structure of This Book

This book is divided into three parts. Part I provides tips, tools, and ideas to "Become a Change Leader." Part II looks at what it takes to "Make Change Happen." Part III helps you think about how to "Maintain the Change" and get your people and organization working in the new way.

This book provides practical advice for achieving results by being a change leader, modeling change resilience, and engaging and inspiring others in a journey that may not always be comfortable or desirable for them. The book is designed both for those who like to read from cover to cover and for those who prefer to dip into sections that interest them. The content will help you think about your organization and determine the best course of action.

Here are some of the topics I will explore:

- Think and act like a change leader.
- Explore the five keys to leading change.
- Motivate and inspire the right actions to build accountability in achieving results.
- Understand the impact a change has on various audiences.
- Accelerate and reinforce the new way.

> Additional resources and free downloads designed to assist you and your team can be found on our website at **www.thetruthaboutchangebook.com**.

May you find a way to bring out your best self in leading yourself and others through these changing times.

PART I

Become a Change Leader

You're braver than you believe,
and stronger than you seem,
and smarter than you think.

—Christopher Robin

Chapter 1

Understand Your Role in Change

Everyone thinks of changing the world, but no one thinks of changing himself.

—Leo Tolstoy

Early in my career, I learned that change is a given. Leaders are trained to think about results. If we want a new result, we must do something different. Innovative solutions and results occur when we figure out how to lead change from idea to result – and how to do it better.

It's often assumed that, if you can lead, you know how to lead change. But being a leader doesn't mean you automatically know how to lead change. It's a skill that is often learned by trial and error. Leading change requires intellectual, emotional, and social intelligence. If you want to achieve results, you must recognize that change is part of an organization's work. Leading change is a leader's prime responsibility; it is not something you can assign to a team, nor is it something you can avoid because you see it as conflict. You are the one who must lead it, and you must engage others in leading their parts in the change.

Leading change has several components: leading yourself, leading others, leading the team, and leading the organization. The people side of change is often overlooked, even though the way to achieve the results you want is by getting people to agree with the approach, align around a solution, and engage in the implementation.

Your actions as a leader are critical to getting people to want to change what they are doing – that is, to understand their role in the change and the results they will create – instead of feeling as if they have to comply. When you are able to engage your people, you can reach your goals and results more quickly.

So much can go wrong in a change initiative that it's not surprising to hear that 70 percent of them fail.

Why?

Perhaps it's because business opportunities are often presented in concrete, linear steps, when change isn't always a linear process. It's much easier to manage the strategic imperative as a cell on a spreadsheet – as a number to be achieved – than to think about how to lead ourselves and others through the change.

Or perhaps it's because we are told, sometimes even commanded, to "just make it happen, and quickly." The whole notion that the results are achieved through the actions of others can be lost in the desire for speedy results. Those results, for which we are accountable, require people, sometimes thousands of them on a global scale, to quickly stop how they were working and switch to a new way.

That's what this book is about: your role as a leader in making the change actually happen in a way that does yield the desired results. We start by looking at your role and at how you can prepare to lead a change initiative.

Prepare for the Transition/Change

In my book *The Executive Transition Playbook: Strategies for Starting Strong, Staying Focused, and Succeeding in Your New Leadership*

Role, I provide a step-by-step process to help incoming leaders navigate their first 100 days in a new role. This same process can be used when leaders prepare to lead a strategic change. The six components in this process help leaders stay focused and grounded in the realities of the situation and can help you prepare to lead the change. Let's take a close look at these six components:

Components to Prepare for Change

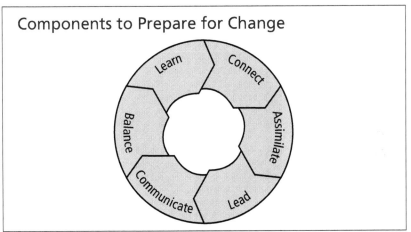

Figure 1-1

Learn

It's easy for you to assume you know enough about the problem and thus miss vital information, cross-organizational challenges, and details that seem trite. Be curious, open up the conversation, and take a 360-degree view of the situation before making decisions or jumping to conclusions.

Knowledge is about having business acumen and understanding the business; about knowing when you need to delve deeper or when you have enough information to make an informed decision. It's about understanding the capability of the organization and doing the best you can to match the right people to the right roles and the right actions to best serve the business and its people. It's also about knowing when you don't have the answers but need to find solutions.

Don't miss the opportunity to learn and get a fresh look at the business before starting to make changes. At the same time, recognize that you may need to make decisions when you do not have all the facts or when the information is ambiguous. There is a balance between collecting enough information and getting so bogged down in information that you avoid making a decision. Engage your leadership team in taking an objective look at the business with you. Assess the business levers and avoid making hasty assumptions based on preconceived notions and biases.

A critical part of this learning is gaining the insights to assess your organization's readiness to change. Some organizations and their people understand that there will be certain change mandates to achieve business targets. Such organizations are ready to change, although they will need the information, directions, and measurements to make sure they are aligned with the change. Other organizations may not see the need for change. Their people may have entrenched positions and may automatically resist what you want to do. Perhaps the leadership team cannot agree on what should be done. You may find in these cases that there is much work to do to gain agreement and alignment before you can implement substantial change.

People can be afraid to express their true feelings about a change for fear their comments could get them into trouble. Instead of fully engaging in the change or expressing their views, people may tell you what they think you want to hear. They may participate in the discussions, but do nothing to implement the change. Learning and understanding the cultural aspects and past experiences with change can help you determine where you may need to dig deeper to understand how to best approach the implementation.

Lead

It can be a mistake for you to assume that you can lead the same way in every situation. New situations require varying leadership behaviors. Change provides a perfect opportunity for you to upgrade and enhance your leadership approach. Too many leaders are afraid to change their own behaviors and therefore miss the opportunity to shed old behaviors and embrace more effective ones.

What you say or do has an impact on what others say and do. You directly create the opportunities or hindrances that affect change initiatives. Change leaders must have the awareness and ability to lead even in the most sensitive situations, with the intention to help, not harm. They must realize that their leadership is only a small part of the entire enterprise and that it takes the entire team to make a difference in the results.

Connect

Business is about interactions and connections. Change leaders value people and relationships. They see their work in terms of relationships, not transactions. Change leaders are interested in and committed to creating and sustaining satisfying and meaningful relationships at work, with family and friends, and in the community.

By connecting with your people, you foster stronger relationships. When your people see you have credibility, they will begin to trust and respect you and will be more apt to follow your lead. They will be more willing to step into new and complex situations because they know that you'll be working alongside them throughout the change process.

Business changes affect both internal and external constituents. You need to connect with stakeholders, both inside and outside the organization. Take the time to listen to their views. Seek their input and incorporate their ideas into the implementation plans. The more you can get others onboard and committed, the sooner the change will happen. By creating a dialogue, you can quickly build mutual trust and respect through open, candid communication, problem-solving, and ongoing actions.

Communicate

Communication is a critical tool, especially during periods of change, when people need more, not less, communication. What you say and do affects how others will or will not engage. You may be keen to share the facts and plans, but people will want you to talk about the impact the change has on them, so that they know the right course of action. Direct communication from you in sound bites that people can hear and digest gives them the information they need and lets you see how your messages are being received and adopted throughout the organization.

If you don't communicate directly with them, people will create their own stories and information. If you *do* communicate directly, you can ensure that accurate messages and information are conveyed to the organization. Timely communication also reduces rumors and keeps the team focused on achieving the business results.

Assimilate

Before initiating a change, you need to understand your company's work styles and cultural norms. Consider how the organization reacts to change, as this can help or hinder the implementation. Assess the organization's prior history with change. While you might think the strategy or plan is new and unique, the organization may see this as yet another initiative doomed to fail. Understand how the organization reacts to changes and what adjustments should be made to enroll and engage the organization to adapt to change.

Balance through Daily Practice

Times of transition can be hectic and stressful, but too may leaders step into a significant change project and try to push right through it. This is not wise. Leading change requires energy and stamina. Unfortunately, daily workouts, family, and personal time can often take a back seat, and finding the right balance isn't always easy, given all your commitments. It is important for your overall health and well-being, as well as the good of the project and organization, for you to be in top shape. Leaders who find ways to follow healthy daily practices stay refreshed and sharp.

More details about how to best use your first 100 days in a transition or period of change can be found in *The Executive Transition Playbook*.

Think Through the Components that Drive Results

As a leader, you may not start out thinking about change. You may see a problem, or better yet an opportunity. You get enamored with the idea of how to achieve a result, and once this idea is formulated, you want to implement it as quickly as you can. Your sense of urgency spikes. You start talking about the opportunity as if it's already happening. You forget that the broader organization has not yet become engaged in the change. Whether you're implementing a new strategy, deploying new processes, merging with another company, or divesting your business, your purpose is to make it easier and more efficient to increase revenues, reduce costs, and command more than your fair share of the market. And after the initial change implementation, you must maintain the change beyond the first uptick in business or a glimmer of a result. It's too easy to declare victory too soon and move onto the next challenge, only to find the results slip.

Consider the following formula for achieving results:

$$\text{IDEAS} + \left(\begin{array}{c} \text{STRATEGY} \\ + \\ \text{PROCESS} \\ + \\ \text{PEOPLE} \end{array}\right) = \text{RESULTS}$$

This change formula includes the following components:

1. Developing the idea and future vision
2. Formulating the best idea into a strategic solution
3. Developing the processes, projects, and initiatives to implement the strategic solution
4. Engaging people in implementing the solution

All four components must be right for you to gain the results you want.

Most leaders are comfortable with leading the first three components. Many leaders, however, aren't ready or able to lead the fourth component: engaging people. They often find themselves running away from the resistances and potential conflicts they encounter when trying to lead change. You need to prepare yourself to be a change leader who can handle and address the people component of change. This requires understanding the timing, cadence, and tempo of the new activities, and also assessing the interdependencies of your change initiative with the other activities going on in the organization.

Become a Change Leader

Change leaders are active in leading initiatives and driving change throughout the organization. Even if you have been leading change for decades, you cannot assume that what worked in the past will work again. Every situation is different, and there are always new things to learn and apply and new issues to address.

Throughout this book, I stress the development of a leader change roadmap (see Chapter 4) that goes beyond the business implementation plan to set out how you will interact with the organization and manage the behavioral side of the change. The most effective change leaders I've worked with prepare themselves to lead the change comprehensively, across all four key components. Here's what they do to prepare themselves.

Inspire a Vision and Commit to the Change

Change is about achieving a vision and a desired outcome. You will want to inspire a vision of what the future can look like. To get to the outcome, you as the leader must commit to the change and then get your people to carry out their parts of the change. This means asking people to commit to doing things differently, doing more of some things and less of others, and adding new actions that may feel awkward and uncomfortable. Some changes may seem easy; others can seem insurmountable. Yet your people must see your personal commitment if they are going to take the risk to change themselves. Timing is critical, as leaders make the trade-offs and juggle the many responsibilities to keep people focused on and committed to the vision.

Set Clear Goals and Outcomes

You as leader lay out what you want to achieve with the change, and you must know how you are going to measure whether the change is achieving its goals. You likely know how to identify and capture the appropriate quantitative measures. The challenge comes in identifying those intermediate, more anecdotal, qualitative measurements. Both types of measurements are needed for you to determine whether the change implementation is on track. Sometimes it helps to ask yourself: "What must I see people doing and saying to know we are on the right track?"

Develop Change Principles and Decision-Making Criteria

It's often assumed leaders will know how to approach change, but this is not always true, especially when multiple leaders are involved in the initiative across layers of the organization. Within a business team, one leader may over-communicate; another may choose not to keep direct reports informed; a third may embellish well beyond the scope of the change. It gets even more complicated with global initiatives and multiple businesses, and with all the leaders wanting to define their own actions. Then, as people talk and share notes, the bits of information they tie together will likely be off-target and lead to unnecessary or unproductive actions.

A core set of change principles and decision-making criteria helps to guide the change initiative. Sound principles provide a consistent approach that you and your people can follow when implementing the change and assessing results. Build your change principles around how you will lead the strategic imperative. This includes strategies and principles to communicate and keep people informed. Determine the level of engagement and communication people can expect from you. Outline your ongoing communication strategy. Your communication principles must take into account the degree of change (high, medium, or low) as well as the difficulty in making the change. Additionally, you may encounter superficial conversations and agreement in meetings, but see no action or follow-up after meetings. Part of supporting people through the change effort is establishing ground rules and principles for engagement and follow-through. Your principles will then give you insights into how much direction and oversight you and your leadership team will need to have to help others.

Recognize that Change Is Personal

We are programmed as leaders to say, "I've got this," and then often find ourselves dealing with our own emotions and challenges in silence. You may feel as if you are on a desert island without any support. Even your friends and colleagues can't help you because they have no idea what you are experiencing. Many times, you'll push this feeling aside as normal stress and wear-and-tear.

People (including you, the leader) are wary of change, as it's personal and about them (and about you). "Will I lose my job?" people ask themselves. "What will happen to my family? What will happen in the future? I don't have another minute in the day to take on anything new." When these personal aspects of change are not addressed, they can surface at the most inopportune times and in ways that aren't supportive to you or others. You must address your reactions to the change so you can help others navigate through it.

Support Others throughout the Change Initiative

People will look for help in figuring out the change, and they will want to talk and ask questions. They are trying to understand what the change means for them, whether they will accept it, and how much personal effort they will need to put into it. If you are leading this initiative, you need to be part of these conversations, so that you can shape the discussions. Sometimes it is helpful to conduct these conversations in a neutral venue off-site where the team will have fewer distractions.

Unfortunately, during times of change, you can be busy and distracted. You may be too worried about other activities and may not spend enough time communicating and engaging others. You may even believe there is nothing more to communicate, so you say nothing. When you are accountable for the results, you are responsible for how people perform to achieve the results. In times of change, you need to be more engaged, fully present, and available. You may need to communicate the same message over and over, at various times, so that people can hear there is no new information. And remember that, if you are not available, people seek colleagues and friends for input, which may not be accurate or useful.

If you are not engaged with your people, they will assume you don't want to hear their concerns. You need to consciously listen and understand the factors that could hinder the very things you want to achieve. You need to engage in objective dialogue repeatedly to enroll key people in the change initiative. Only then will you gain the commitment and get the people engaged in those consistent actions that will take the organization from its current state to the future results.

Lead the Change

There is a difference between managing and leading. It's easy to get them confused, as most roles include both management and leadership components. Managing requires engaging people in what is known. Leading is about figuring out what people need to do to make change happen. Managing is about building to consistency, while leading is about navigating to something new and different. Leadership implies accountability, which means ensuring that there is commitment to the change and that the changes are being implemented by both the leader and those in the organization.

You may struggle with implementation. You may have a hard time connecting with the organization to get a good view of how the change is progressing. Or you may not believe that paying attention to the people component really matters. But implementation implies leading your people to get results, and includes reinforcing new behaviors and processes to maintain the results. *You* must take action to lead the change.

When I look at change initiatives, I often see very decent project plans and even some organizational readiness plans that contain communication and training. What is usually missing, though, is an understanding of the behaviors required first by leaders and then by individuals to implement the change. It's often assumed that if an activity is in the project plan, and the project plan is approved by leadership, the change will magically occur. It's assumed that if people are trained, they will automatically start working in the new way. But that's not how it happens. Often, the activities in the implementation plans and training are not carried out. There is a tendency for people to do the activities that provide them positive reinforcement and avoid activities that are uncomfortable. To get the new behaviors started requires a clear plan that includes the behavioral changes needed to perform in the new way. The leadership discussions, coaching, mentoring, and feedback – the people side of change – all must be laid out in the leader change roadmap plan. A leader change roadmap (see Chapter 4) guides you in how to lead the change, from the initial discussions through the implementation of an initiative.

Demonstrate Change Resiliency

It can be hard for you as a leader and for your people to take on something new when you are holding tightly onto old practices and beliefs. This takes letting go of the old practices and beliefs to implement the change. You need the insight to manage the emotional, mental, and physical reactions to the challenges, opportunities, and setbacks in ways that take into consideration what the people and the business need.

Resilient leaders have the compassion to listen, work to enroll others, and demonstrate the courage to stay the course for the good of the enterprise. Resilient leaders are flexible and adaptable and know when to implement specific changes. They are able to create a foundation for others and can move quickly when the situation changes. Resilient leaders are able to make sense of fluctuating situations and can infuse both energy and creativity to achieve positive outcomes.

Here are a few things to consider as you build your change resiliency and move toward becoming an effective change leader:

◆ Respect the growing pains associated with change.
◆ Recognize that emotions are part of the change process. What one person sees as a significant change may be a non-event to another.
◆ Develop your own resiliency and change behaviors first.
◆ Be a positive force for the change. Create a structure but be flexible to make adjustments, with an eye always on the results.
◆ Get comfortable with the ambiguous nature of change.

CHANGE LEADERSHIP ACTIONS

- Inspire a vision and commit to change.
- Set clear goals and outcomes.
- Develop change principles and decision-making criteria.
- Recognize that change is personal. People may need more information and support to process and accept the situation.
- Support others throughout the change initiative by creating an environment and sufficient positive feedback to reinforce new behaviors.
- Lead the change by identifying and reinforcing the new behaviors you want to see.
- Demonstrate change resiliency to infuse energy and creativity for positive outcomes.

Figure 1-2

Questions I Ask Change Leaders

When I work with my clients, we discuss what it takes to lead change. I ask them to think about the following questions to make sure they are truly assessing the situation and determining where they are headed. Then, they develop their change goals and engage others who can help them make it happen. Take the time now to answer these questions. After you have your own answers, you can discuss these items with your leadership team to ensure that you are all in agreement. As you answer these questions, pay attention to the impact your leadership actions will have on others. Then you can make adjustments to achieve successful outcomes.

Do You Understand What's at Stake?

It's one thing to have a solution; it's another to understand the risks and what's actually at stake. Are you committed to leading yourself and others through the change, regardless of what you need to deal with? Do you understand what the change means for your organization and for all your people? What ambivalence or concerns do you have that you may not be verbalizing? What are your preconceived notions or even blind spots about how the change will affect you, the business, the people, or the organization's culture? Most solutions become very complicated; how can you simplify the solution into concepts that everyone can understand?

Are You Willing to Do What It Takes to Make This a Success?

Is there a clear plan? How will you measure success? What commitments will you make to leading the change, even if you face significant resistance and politics? What are the three to five specific goals you want to accomplish during this change? How do your own behaviors, priorities, and actions need to change to achieve the results you want?

How Will You Get Others Committed and Engaged in the Change?

When people are spread too thin and are operating outside their comfort zone, they may retreat and do nothing until they assess the risk to themselves. Know which key stakeholders you need to engage in implementing the change. Understand how people will react to the change. Think through scenarios of how people may react and imagine what questions they may have. Create a sense of urgency to get others engaged and moving in the right direction. Have you built trust and respect with others, so that they are willing to let you lead them in the change? Use the change as a vehicle to build commitment to action.

What Do You Need to Do to Lead This Change?

Understand your leadership strengths and vulnerabilities, so you can assess how well you will lead change. Be honest. Most leaders are not prepared for or comfortable with leading change. Their insecurities play out in their actions. Some push ahead, while others hide in their shells like turtles. Some may get angry and frustrated, and others may become paralyzed and stall. As you prepare for the change, remind yourself that you yourself may be uncomfortable working in new ways; however, these new actions are exactly what the organization needs from you. Ask yourself: "What leadership skills and behaviors will be necessary to perform at the highest level? How will I approach this change while juggling the other aspects of my role? What do people need to hear to want to follow my lead?"

When the Going Gets Tough, How Will You Motivate Yourself and Others?

When the change is announced, there is typically a surge of activity. Then it's time to take steps to implement the solution. At some point, the implementation becomes difficult, as people struggle with doing things differently. Look at your implementation plan and determine those critical points in the project. How will you continue to lead the change in the face of issues? How will you handle the setbacks and, more importantly, how will you celebrate the small, possibly insignificant, victories to keep people moving toward the goals?

When the going gets tough, it's easy to focus on what's not working. But this is precisely the time to point out what *is* working, so you can inspire others as they work in a new way. You need to provide additional positive feedback and carefully use constructive feedback to encourage people to develop new skills. Many times, obstacles and impediments will get in the way. Help people work around them or eliminate those barriers so you can all keep moving toward the goal. Ask yourself:

◆ Am I being objective, or am I so focused on the results that I am missing something?

◆ Do I have enough knowledge about the business, the key stakeholders, and the organization to be able to execute the change effectively?

◆ Is my judgment clouded by what I think the change should be?

◆ Have I earned the trust and respect of the organization to lead the change?

◆ How will these relationships be tested in the months ahead?

◆ What will it take to bring out the best in me and in others?

> If you go to **www.thetruthaboutchangebook.com** and click on "Free Book Bonuses," you will find a list of change-leader readiness questions in a printable format.

Do You Understand the Difference between Change Leadership and Change Management?

This question gets to the core of what makes a change initiative a success, a partial success, or a failure. In this book, we will talk about change leadership and about how leaders engage and lead change. This is different from change management, which is a set of processes, tools, and techniques for controlling and keeping a change effort on track.

Too often, I see leaders delegating the deployment of an initiative to the change management team, taking themselves out of the implementation and only becoming available for oversight and when things go off track. Instead, I prefer to see leaders taking a more active role by creating change leadership strategies and devising a leader change roadmap, especially when tricky behavioral changes are needed. Unfortunately, as soon as change is discussed, people think about "change management" and not about "change leadership." So much energy goes into creating organizational plans that the leadership actions often are not addressed. If you consider these terms to be the same, you will likely not get the business outcomes you want.

Change leadership is different. Change leadership provides a way for leaders to think, strategize, plan, and take action, especially about how they will lead and execute the strategies and plans. Change leadership consists of getting leaders to become involved. Change leadership takes into account the whole business ecosystem, the business levers that are affected when one part of the business changes, and how the changes affect the overall business culture and outcomes. It links ideas, strategies, processes, and people to results.

Leaders create success by doing what is needed to thoroughly implement a strategic initiative. The actions you take as a change leader in relation to your leadership team and people create the culture in which the change can actually lead to the results you want – the new normal.

When you take the change leadership actions in Figure 1-2 – when you prepare to lead change consciously with awareness of your impact on leading and implementing change – you accelerate the change process and move your company toward achieving its goals. You take your company and your people beyond what they thought was possible and together you reap the results. In future chapters, we will discuss these topics more deeply, to provide a framework for leading change successfully.

Key Takeaways from Chapter 1

1. Leading change means leading yourself, others, the team, and the organization. Prepare for the change by gaining the knowledge, making the connections, and determining how to lead.

2. Review and address the four elements that drive results, as shown in this formula:

Ideas + Strategy + Process + People = Results

You must manage all components to get the results you want.

3. Become a change leader by using the actions in Figure 1-2.

4. Work through the change readiness questions to prepare to lead change. Achieve the results you want by answering these change questions:

- Do you understand what's at stake?

- Are you willing to do whatever it takes to make this a success?

- How will you get others committed and engaged in the change?

- What do you need to do to lead this change?

- When the going gets tough, how will you motivate yourself and others?

Chapter 2

Understand Your Organization and Its People

Out of the clutter, find simplicity.

—*Albert Einstein*

When you are developing a change initiative, you can easily focus on the business plan and the problems you are trying to solve, without trying to understand the impact of your changes on others throughout the organization. You may be working from your business perspective, but because change initiatives depend on people and teams, you need to understand how *they* see the change. You may assume that they will accept and agree with what you want them to do, although they may have different perspectives.

For example, you develop the business case with the results in mind. Perhaps the wording in the business case is not clear, and there is room for interpretation. Your people may start implementing from their perspectives, which may not be aligned with yours. You have just increased the likelihood that the organizational actions will fall short. Instead, you need to think in terms of how your organization and its people think, interpret, and act, so you can make your change initiative successful.

The Scope of the Change

The dynamics of change shift when you look at it from different perspectives – leading the organization, leading the teams (business groups and functions), leading others, and leading yourself. In chapter 1 we discussed leading yourself and becoming a change leader. Let's take a look at the other three perspectives of leading change.

The Organization

At the organization level, the entire business ecosystem, along with all business components, merges to form a whole. This is the usual starting point for most changes. At this level, you can have clarity about the vision, results, and high-level plans. It is imperative to be aware, though, that there is a potential for lack of understanding, coordination, and alignment, especially where different business units and functions implement the change at different rates. So it is critical to recognize how your changes in some areas affect work in other areas across the organization.

The Teams

Organization-level changes are implemented by different business units, functional teams, and departments. You must understand the dynamics of how each area works and how they all work together, including relationships among key personnel, patterns of influence, and workflow. Business units, functions, and departments can have their own sets of work dynamics that may not be conducive to cross-organizational changes.

People

People carry out the specific, physical actions, and they need clarity around roles, tasks, and key behaviors to do their work as you want. The impact of the change (physically, mentally, and emotionally) will dictate how quickly people engage in the change and how well they carry out their assigned actions.

All four perspectives – the organization, the teams, the people, and yourself – must be considered. You may find that you cannot visualize

Figure 2-1

the work at or between each of these levels. If this is the case, you may not be able to provide the direction needed; instead, your direction may be confusing or may miss the mark entirely. You may not be comfortable leading change at the people level, but if you do not pay attention to your people, you may run into resistance, lack of understanding, or incorrect actions.

Think about what you need to accomplish both in relation to the organization (at the organization, team, and people levels) and in relation to your organization's people. Your plans must work for both, and you must think in terms of implementing for both. Chapter 8 provides more information on how to lead change from the perspective of the organization, the team, and the individual.

The Organization

Organizations are often interested in minimizing disruption and maintaining the organization as it is. This may interfere with the ability to maximize results through executing your change plan.

During a period of change, successful organizations prepare senior management, engage key influencers, and help employees understand any change through consistent and timely communications. Such successful organizations go beyond role definition and identify the new behaviors and consequence systems that make the solution work efficiently. There may be consequences and implications you are not aware of. Even with a solid business case, there are pros and cons, as well as opportunities and risks. Those trade-offs need to be considered, along with the impact of an organization-wide strategic initiative on business areas. When the strategic implications are considered, you can determine where deployment needs to be consistent and where certain areas may need to be adjusted.

Successful organizations take the following into account when implementing changes:

1. Developing a compelling reason for change and presenting a business case that individuals will want to become part of
2. Creating a leader change roadmap, which plots the appropriate leadership strategies and actions that will drive and reinforce the new behaviors and processes
3. Communicating through clear, compelling messages customized for each group of stakeholders
4. Engaging key stakeholders by removing obstacles to peak performance and building positive reinforcement systems
5. Enlisting and enrolling the full leadership team in the implementation changes and processes

The key is to create an implementation strategy that captures both what you need to get done and how you want the organization and its people to work.

CHANGE LEADERSHIP ACTIONS

- Recognize how your change initiative will affect work throughout the organization, not just at the site of change.
- Learn about the dynamics of how your organization's business units and key personnel interact.
- Think through how your change initiative will affect your leadership team and your people.
- Develop a compelling business case for change that people will want to implement.
- Assess the types of communications, conversations, and interpersonal actions you need to make to get your organization and its people on board.
- Understand what you need to do to lead your organization and its people through the change and to enable others to make the change happen.
- Prepare the organization, so that you get the results you want.

Figure 2-2

The Organization's People

Human capital is by far the best asset a company has to implement strategic initiatives. An investment in the right human capital takes a company from where it is today into the future. The organizations that can engage their people and align their work to the change initiative will achieve their goals more efficiently and faster. This requires understanding the impacts of change on the people in the organization. Creating thoughtful engagement plans can make the difference between success and failure.

Change initiatives often fail in implementation. What happens? Either the direction to the people wasn't clear, or there wasn't enough buy-in to gain momentum for the changes. Sometimes people resist, hold out, and wait. For example, one company implemented a new sales approach, but the very people who were supposed to use the new approach were those who said, "This is just another one of those programs. The president is new and will not last more than a few years. I'll wait and see before implementing the sales approach."

Some may think that resorting to cycles of rewards and punishment or using a command-and-control approach will elicit the desired behaviors. Unfortunately, while these methods may seem to yield some forward action, over time, people catch on to these approaches, and their actions become erratic and inconsistent. The key is to give people a purpose and reason underlying their work, along with the reinforcement that encourages new actions.

You might be fortunate enough to have resources to charter a project team and even a change management team to handle the changes. You may have a change-savvy human resources team to address the people aspects, including communications, training, onboarding, and transitions. These support systems create plans to enable leaders. However, leaders are accountable for crafting the change strategies and conducting the day-to-day conversations. Messages are cascaded from leader to performer. If these behavioral communications don't work, people cannot perform their part in making change happen.

People Are a Critical Asset

With the stakes so high, it is critical for leaders to assess how people are being used. As you consider the people in your company, ask yourself:

- Do you have the right "people strategy" to implement the change?
- Is your leadership team equipped to lead the change?
- What will it take to get your leadership team and the people ready?
- What can you do right now to better leverage the discretionary effort of the leadership team and the people in your organization?

Your answers will tell you which investments in human capital you need to make before you can take your company from where it is today into the future.

How People React to Change

Change, by definition, means "to make or become different." Synonyms for change include: alter, adjust, adapt, amend, modify, revise, refine. When you implement change, you are asking your people to act and behave differently; you are asking them to alter, adjust, and adapt to a new way of working. As the people try to understand physically, mentally, emotionally, and spiritually what the change means to them, they may resist it.

Before they are willing to make significant changes, they will want to know whether it's worth putting time and effort into the new activity. They desire evidence and facts that the plans have a high likelihood of success. They are assessing the level of difficulty and the risk and rewards involved.

We are all familiar with the typical frustrations when trying something new:

- The work is different, and people feel they lack the competence and capability to effectively and efficiently carry out the work.

- The new activity is confusing and difficult to perform. It is almost painful to get through the activity, all the time wondering if the activity is worth it.

- There are bottlenecks, conflicting priorities, and faulty schedules. Handoffs from one individual to another aren't working properly. Colleagues become frustrated with one another. People don't have the time to perform all the actions, so work is left undone.

- Leaders may have announced the changes, yet they are not present to help solve challenges as they arise. People are left to make their own decisions.

Even hearing the word "change" can create stress for almost anyone who has experienced a change initiative that went off course. The more experienced people learn to wait and see what happens. Everyone becomes very careful about how they invest their energy. Their experience tells them not to step into just any situation, with just any leader. They know that certain conditions need to be met to ensure that a change initiative will be successful.

Resistances and Fear

Change scares most people. When people hear about a significant change, they may experience physical, mental, emotional, and spiritual reactions, and may even find core beliefs challenged. (I use the word "spiritual" to mean the person's energy, beliefs, motivation, and personal choice.) It is normal to resist change. Such resistance is a signal to pay attention and to identify and address the causes of the resistance. Ask "What's this all about? Is there a problem? How should I handle this?"

People always want to know what the change means *for them*. Your people are assessing, "Will this change help or harm me? Can I perform and succeed, or will I fail?" We're conditioned not to fail; it's better to avoid any negative experiences than to fail. The fear of failure can easily make people hold out and wait. Even a beneficial change can be met with skepticism. Each person is deciding what's in it for them and estimating the amount of energy and effort that will be needed to execute the changes. Sometimes, people decide to hold back or to resist moving forward.

People need to know whether risk taking is endorsed and whether it is safe to try new approaches. If people take risks and fail, will they be fired? Some businesses are set up to try new approaches and even to fail fast when seeking the best solutions. Other organizations say they want the best ideas, but stifle creativity. When people pick up that there are negative consequences for failing, they will play it safe. Leaders create the environment. If you aren't getting the results you want, you should look at what you and other leaders are doing or saying and how that drives behavior.

Why "Just Do It" Is a Lousy Engagement Strategy

Too often, a change is announced, and the leadership team expects the organization to jump into action. To you, the solution and actions may be obvious, and you may tell your people to "just do it." This is naïve when the solution and actions may not be obvious.

"Just do it" assumes that people have bought into the idea, the goal, and the purpose. "Just do it" assumes people are capable and motivated to carry out the new actions.

In times of change, though, the people may not be ready or may not have bought into the idea. They may lack the ability to make the changes. As the leader, your role is to prepare the organization, to coach and guide it to achieve new results, and to coach and support the people doing the work. For a "just do it" strategy to work in business, the components needed to help others train, perform, and succeed must already be in place. A "just do it" strategy requires behavior changes from all parts of the organization – and it starts with the leaders.

The Change Leader in the Organization

Leading a change initiative is tricky, because you are asking people to do something different to achieve a different result. Change is a series of behaviors linked together to arrive at a result. The change goes beyond conceptual thinking to a series of linked behaviors and actions leading to the desired result. It requires people to adjust their behaviors and to work through their resistances and fears. Your job is to find a way to lead people through the change so they can do their best, most productive work.

People look to you for direction, guidance, and support. During change, though, you can get tied up in meetings and strategy implementation and may forget that your most important priority should be enabling your people. You may also be consumed with your personal reactions and challenges. Acting like a change leader is less about what *you* want and need and more about enabling *others* to do whatever they need to make the change happen.

To lead change successfully takes a commitment to become fully engaged in leading in a new way. The use of a leader change roadmap (see Chapter 4) incorporates the project implementation plan and the leadership plan to enable new behaviors to be implemented.

Remember this truth: People are a strategic component in deploying the change. People are the key to achieving the results, in any company, industry, or location. When the people side of change is not managed, initiatives cannot achieve their goals and may even fail.

A Holistic Perspective Helps

A large multinational launched a new global strategy. Its plans included several key acquisitions. The leadership team had all collaborated on the strategy. However, the CEO quickly learned that leaders were implementing the strategy in very different ways, causing confusion across the divisions and functions.

Upon further examination, the CEO heard different perspectives that had not surfaced in the creation of the strategy:

◆ The CFO was concerned that the recent acquisition projections were overstated. She was hoping that the business had a solid plan to make up for the recent loss of a key piece of business.

◆ Divisional and functional leaders saw the sheer number of "priorities" pulling people in different directions. One leader said, "My team hasn't completed the actions from last month's initiative kickoffs. We are under pressure to make the quarter's numbers with targets that aren't realistic, given the loss of a major customer and product stock outs."

◆ Many people were pulled into the integration planning of the acquisition of a key competitor. The integration manager was baffled why it was so difficult for the people to complete their integration action items. From her perspective, delivering on the synergies was critical to the new global strategy, so she was frustrated that the leaders who were part of the integration planning process were falling short on key milestones.

♦ The human resources leader continued to be optimistic: "We have developed a series of events to engage people. We are working on better role definition, which caused some confusion, and the recent compensation and benefits changes were very well received."

♦ Employees didn't seem to say much; there were few questions in the recent town hall meeting. Behind the scenes, people were overwhelmed. They felt underappreciated and kept in the dark until the last minute. They saw their leaders were distracted and only heard from them when something was wrong. One person said, "I like my manager, but he is so busy, I don't want to bother him."

The CEO said, "How hard can it be to deliver the number? We agreed as a leadership team to the strategy. I am disappointed; I told my team we can't miss another number. We are losing credibility with the board and the marketplace."

The CEO recognized that each perspective provided a different set of information and lens for leading the business. The CEO decided the leadership team needed to take a more holistic view of all the initiatives to prioritize and sequence key actions and map out a go-forward plan that worked in concert with each business and function.

The leadership team met to discuss the initiatives and identify critical actions. It wasn't an easy conversation, as leaders had different perspectives. The discussions enabled the leaders to look at the various perspectives and align around how they would talk with one consistent voice to the organization. They mapped out a set of common principles and developed actions that were aligned to the priorities. Their plans were socialized, and other personnel were engaged to provide input. The execution of the strategy became a collaborative effort.

The holistic view of the business components helped to streamline and simplify the actions. The leaders were able to craft actions and messages to fit the perspectives. Leaders became more engaged in the implementation at the right times, and they committed to ongoing oversight of the strategic initiatives beyond the typical reporting. As a result of this new organizational alignment, the business was able to set a path to deliver the results using the strategy.

Key Takeaways in Chapter 2

1. Change happens from four perspectives: yours, the people's, the teams', and the organization's. Be aware of and understand the needs of all four perspectives to enable all aspects of a change effort.

2. Successful organizations plan for change by developing a compelling business case for the change, enlisting the leadership team, and engaging key stakeholders in implementing the change.

3. Human capital is an organization's best asset in implementing change. People need to understand how the change will affect them, what they have to do to implement the change, and what results they are expected to deliver.

4. Leaders must be prepared to deal with people's resistances and fears in periods of change. This may mean providing them the support to work through the physical, mental, emotional, and spiritual aspects of implementing new behaviors.

Chapter 3

Build Your Case for Change

It's not enough to stare up the steps;
we must step up the stairs.

—Vaclav Havel

People want the positive results change can bring, but don't want to be told to change. In business, we are constantly asking people to change for the good of the organization. Meanwhile, people want to come to work to carry out their craft and perfect their skills. They need to be persuaded to change and reassured that their skills will still be valued during and after the change.

Start with the Business Plan

Business strategies and plans capture the ideas and solutions. A business plan focuses on the challenges, financial implications, and strategies for creating value and growth. Many business plans have the same structure: They start with a one-page summary that includes the vision and a set of pillars to represent the key areas of focus; the pages that follow usually go into detail about each pillar. The plans contain a wealth of information, with pages and pages providing deep analysis with specific facts and data, and reviewing financials and competitive and market analyses. Through the many tables, charts, and figures, you give a picture of what you think needs to be added or changed to improve the business. Such a business plan provides a sense of the business landscape and information necessary for you to present your big picture of the business and to gain approval of the plan from others, such as the Board of Directors and the leadership team.

Convert Your Business Plan into a Powerful Case for Change

It can be tempting to try to use the business plan as the communication vehicle to enroll others in your solution and gain alignment. This is a mistake. The business plan is usually too focused on the business and doesn't take into account the behavioral aspects of making the change happen. Often, the business plan is not well articulated. The plan may be put together by strategy and consultant teams and take an organizational top-down view of the business. There is so much information that the underlying issues in the organization – the ones leading to the need for change – are buried.

There is so much information in the typical business plan that conversations about it turn into monologues, with leaders telling people about the details in the plan. When leaders ask for comments and reactions, they may be met with silence and glazed-over eyeballs. The information rarely gets converted into something that better articulates and creates a conversation around the path forward. Silence becomes "agreement." Leaders are so familiar with the information that it may be hard to figure out how to develop the right messages or convert the plan into a dialogue.

Usually, business plans do not speak about how the business interactions and culture may be contributing to the problem or about how the leaders need to act differently to execute the plan. Other initiatives may crowd out this one. Developing a case for change as a companion to the business plan forces you to consider the degree of change, the organization's capabilities and culture, and the risks involved in making such a change. A case for change enables the leaders to succinctly articulate the what, why, when, where, and how that can bring a business plan to life.

A powerful case for change communicates a vision of why the change is needed in words that help those making the changes "want" to be part of this solution. It projects why it is worth putting in the effort to achieve the desired outcomes. It clarifies the scope of the initiative, and describes the journey from the current ways of working to the future that will provide positive results to the business, markets, and customers. The case for change helps to address the questions and concerns people will naturally have and prepares leaders to discuss the initiative in terms that people can hear. Most of the time, people just see a change initiative as another set of tasks that have been piled onto their plate. A common reaction from people can be: "No, we can't take this on. This will not work. Not now." The case for change works to tie the whole story together and to find positive outcomes for employees to engage in the change.

In developing a case for change, you need to review and assess the ability and tolerance levels of the organization in taking on the initiative. You can then see what's needed to make the change work, and you can set out the messages to help people understand the direction and know how they will be involved. When you present your case for change to your people, they will be assessing what is being asked of them for this new initiative. They will want to prioritize, sort, and sequence what they do and how much emphasis to put on this new program. They will be thinking through the interdependencies with other activities.

Figure 3-1 outlines a set of questions for you and your team to use to convert the business plan into a case for change. Leaders often overlook the need to talk with the leadership team about how to communicate the business case; but this conversation is necessary for planning how to communicate to help others understand, process, and take action on the information.

Questions for Creating a Case for Change

1. Define the current situation that needs to change. How are people delivering the results today?
2. What does the future look like? What will people do and say?
3. If the plan works, what will it look like?
4. Why is it important to make this change now?
5. What are the priorities?
6. What roadblocks and risks may get in our way?
7. How will we measure success?
8. How will we get from the current state to the future?
9. How will we sequence this effort with the other activities under way?
10. What do we all need to do to make this successful?

Figure 3-1

A case for change is used repeatedly in the progression from idea to solution to implementation: to gain agreement from the leadership team; to start the work of the project team; and to announce the changes to the organization. The case for change is often referred to during the implementation process to keep everyone focused and moving in the right direction. It's a reminder of the journey from the current state to the future and of how success will be measured.

Get Clear About the Goals, Measurements, and WIIFM (What's in It for Me?)

A strong case for change outlines where the organization is and where it is going. It links the solution to the outcome and sets out what is involved in the implementation. The case for change includes both quantitative and qualitative goals as the measurements of success. While quantitative measures provide important data, qualitative measures give a texture of "how" the organization is engaged and being led through the change.

Engage the leadership team in setting both quantitative and qualitative goals. Outline milestone points so that you and your team know that you are headed in the right direction. What evidence and what actions should you be seeing if the initiative is moving ahead? Be clear with people how you will measure this progress so that they know what to expect. Go one step further and think about the key stakeholders involved; can you capture what is in it for them if they participate fully? Answer the question on everyone's mind: "Why should I put my full energy and attention into this project?"

CHANGE LEADERSHIP ACTIONS

- Build a business plan to gain approval of the strategic initiative.
- Convert your business plan into a case for change to gain the support of your leadership team and people.
- Gain clarity around goals and measurements.
- Use the Leader Change Roadmap to work with your organization and people.
- Identify your key stakeholders and work to gain their acceptance.

Figure 3-2

Five Keys to Leading Change

Change takes businesses and people out of their comfort zone. Some people like it, but most would prefer doing things the way they always have done, even when it's clear that change is needed. These people will wait until it is necessary before they change. Sometimes, when they are asked if they want changes, they will say "yes," but when asked to make the change, they may not be as interested. Sometimes businesses resist change by waiting until revenue slips and targets are missed, and then the changes needed are massive and dire. These businesses delay until business results are so off target that change is the only option. Both people and businesses want to stay with known ways of working, rather than trying new approaches, but often change is needed, and leaders want to change their organizations.

Over my years of working with leaders, I have identified five keys to leading change, which I call the Leader Change Framework (see Figure 3-3). Let's look closely at these keys.

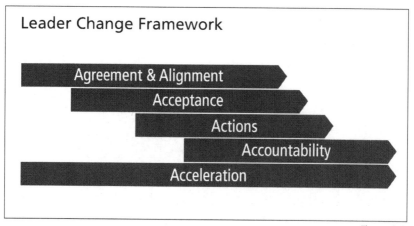

Figure 3-3

Accountability

When you accept accountability for the results of a change, you chart a direction and model new behaviors. You own the solution and are responsible for taking the appropriate actions. You communicate, coach, and provide feedback to create resiliency throughout the organization. Your role is to help people see why they need to take action now. Often the initiative benefits the business, but it may not be perceived as actually aiding the people or other stakeholders. You need to educate people about the initiative from various perspectives, so they understand what will happen and how the changes will be deployed. You are responsible for inspiring others with a compelling vision to engage in the actions. There are usually a handful of new behaviors that are critical to the operation that may not naturally occur without some oversight, coaching, and reinforcement from leadership. Knowing where the sticking points will be and addressing them early can keep the plans moving forward. This is all part of accountability.

Times of change require focus and intermediate targets (milestones) to keep people and teams moving ahead. People may not naturally start to take accountability for their parts of the solution and implementation, unless you set out how they can "own" their work. Teams may not see themselves as accountable unless you build accountability into their mandates and measure their accomplishments in moving toward the change goals.

I've seen steering committees engage in project reviews only on a transactional basis, thereby avoiding their role in making the change happen. They criticize the plans. They blame others for the implementation challenges. They may tell others to fix the problems; but these leaders have distanced themselves from the problems.

Their lack of ownership and action contributes to the issues with deployment. Months later, it should be no surprise that the lack of leadership accountability has caused the initiative to fail.

Agreement & Alignment

Leadership teams often struggle to gain consensus about what to do or alignment around implementing the strategic initiative.

Agreement. Functional or departmental leaders may see the change from different perspectives. Organizational politics or agendas can inhibit agreement. Without full agreement, it's difficult to implement a consistent direction. There can be differing agendas, politics, priorities, and views of the world. People don't intend to disagree, but this disagreement when it's not addressed can cause issues during the implementation process. It can create confusion throughout the organization as leaders implement the initiative at different times and cadences.

Gain Agreement of Your Leadership Team. Gaining agreement starts with having an open dialogue about the case for change. The dialogue sets out what needs to change, why it's important, and how success will be measured. With agreement, the leadership team works to form a common opinion and set of actions to achieve the business goals. To some, this will sound obvious. In practice, few leadership teams truly agree on key issues. Some wait for the senior leader to make a decision. Others give the concept lip service, but behind the scenes nothing really happens.

Successful implementation starts with a leadership team's agreeing on the direction. These leadership teams work through the differences that inhibit implementing solutions. They surface perspectives, test decisions, and assess risk tolerances early on. When these teams aren't in agreement around the strategy and why it's important to take on this work, it creates confusion throughout the organization. The change implementation is stalled because the leaders are setting numerous directions within their respective areas. People either do nothing, or they do what they feel is the right thing to do. Either way, the actions hinder the result.

On the path to agreement, some leaders are silenced by their boss or peers. Others jockey for position or push their own agenda, which may derail strategic imperatives. Sometimes leaders move quickly to implement something – anything – without agreeing on what they're implementing

Here are steps for gaining the agreement of your leadership team.

1. **Be Clear and Focused:** Be clear and focused about what you want to gain agreement around and how you will get people to agree.
2. **Gather the Information:** Pull together all the information necessary to discuss the initiative and make a decision. This is where the case for change is useful, as long as it looks at various perspectives. Too often, a case for change is skewed to the decision a leader wants to reach and misses alternative solutions.
3. **Be Objective:** It's easy to make a decision before considering all sides of an issue. Remain objective, let go of any preconceived notions, and look at all sides of the situation. Some participants may not speak up as readily as others. To get to the right answer, make sure that everyone's voice is heard.
4. **Make a Decision:** Determine how the ultimate decision will be made. Ensure that you have had enough conversation and have looked at different scenarios. As you start to arrive at possible options, be sure to assess the pros and cons of each. At some point, the team will be ready to make a decision. Once the decision is made, test that it holds up. Sometimes it helps to ask

members of the team to explain the decision. This often surfaces different interpretations of the decision and exposes cracks in the agreement.

5. **Uphold the Decision:** The discussion can get heated, but once the decision is made, unless it is unethical or illegal, uphold it. The team should act as one voice outside the room.

Alignment. Agreement doesn't always mean alignment. Agreement is about "what" you want to do and "why" it is important. Alignment is about "how" a group will carry out the direction or next steps to deploy the strategy. Having different agendas, big egos, and competing priorities can get in the way of achieving both agreement and alignment.

Agreement is an acknowledgment about the business information. It doesn't mean that people will take action. Leaders may agree that something needs to happen, but they may not be aligned around the desired outcomes, why it's important, or how to implement the change. When departments and functions rely on handoffs, the lack of alignment around a consistent implementation plan can mean mistakes and extra work. People get frustrated. Take the time to gain agreement both on what you want to do and on why you think it is necessary so that you can gain alignment around how to carry out the solution.

We've all seen what can happen when the various members of a leadership team are not in agreement or aligned. They walk through the motions, only to keep things moving along. Later in the implementation phase, these leaders aren't fully engaged in the deployment of the initiative. They are late on deliverables. They miss meetings. Each functional area may have a different interpretation of the problem and which direction to take. They may be in the midst of other initiatives and may not want to take on an initiative that could be a distraction.

Nothing kills change more than lack of alignment. Without alignment, some members of the leadership team may feel they have the license to approach the change as they choose.

Acceptance

As we have discussed, change scares people and triggers fear. For people to move forward, they may need to process the change mentally, emotionally, physically, and spiritually. People will want to know what's going to happen to them and why it's important to make the changes now. People need safe places to talk about their concerns and to discuss how they will engage in new actions without feeling vulnerable.

Having all the facts, logic, and plans may still not be enough for people to want to engage in the change. Often, the path toward acceptance starts with the leader and perhaps a small team. At first, the team may even show some resistance or doubt about the change. The more discussions, the more the team gets convinced and comfortable that this is the right thing to do. I've even seen teams start to talk about the change as if it had already occurred, ignoring the fact that there is bound to be resistance when the change is communicated to the organization.

Once the change has been fleshed out, it's time to start building acceptance by getting others involved. People will have reservations and be defensive. It will take a compelling reason to change and a consistency of leadership actions to get people quickly onboard. If there is any confusion after the announcement, people will go back to the pile of work that awaits them. They may consult a colleague and begin to put together a story, which may not even be built on facts. Before the initiative is under way, people will be discounting and readjusting their contribution.

Your role is to get people engaged and committed to the change. It means helping people understand what will happen, why it's important, and what they are to do.

Gain Acceptance from Key Stakeholders. You can support key stakeholders by helping them navigate the mental, emotional, and physical aspects of the change. It's not about forcing, pushing, or maneuvering people to change. Rather, it's about providing the information and context, so that people can process the information and make the right choices to positively engage in change. The case for change provides the business information to navigate from the current to the future state.

A Stakeholder Conversation Plan converts the business plan and case for change into material for a conversation with an individual or a group of people. Such a plan is a powerful way to approach the conversation from the individual's perspective instead of merely telling people what's going to happen. To create your Stakeholder Conversation Plan, work through the questions in Figure 3-4. This approach provides an objective, fact-filled, informed way to prepare for these conversations. It takes into account how the people will react, it asks you to think about what people need to know, and it takes a strategic approach to engaging people. As people get their questions answered and as you remove the concerns, then moving from resisting the idea to accepting the idea can happen. People understand why they are committing to the change and can therefore accelerate the outcomes.

Your project team may start the work of developing the Stakeholder Conversation Plan, but the real work of gaining agreement and acceptance falls on your shoulders. This work becomes easier if you get people involved early in the conversations about the goals

---

Questions for Creating a Stakeholder Conversation Plan

- ◆ Who is important to implementing this change? This may be an individual or a group of people.
- ◆ What do you want this individual or group to know?
- ◆ How do you wish them to feel about the messages?
- ◆ What actions will you need them to take?
- ◆ What resistance, concerns, or reactions could be encountered as you proceed?
- ◆ What is the best way to get this individual or group of people excited and engaged?
- ◆ What actions are needed by you or others to assist the individual or group?

Figure 3-4

and actions. Spend time planning what you will communicate and how you will deliver the messages, even when you feel there isn't any new information. People will react to the messages. Anticipate and understand their reactions so that you can engage in the right conversations to help keep people from getting stuck. The more that people can keep moving ahead, the sooner that you will reach the goal.

Actions

As you observe people reacting to your communications and messages, ask yourself, "What can I do or say that will help my colleagues process the information and take action?" Often people first need to process what they heard to understand the impact on them. Then they need to determine how they will take action. In that process, they may get stuck and may require more reinforcement as they begin to try things in a new way.

Too few leaders like to prepare for these conversations. Those who do, find they have more productive conversations with their people. If leaders avoid these conversations, the issues begin to fester and confusion and conflict increases. During times of change, there will be contrasting opinions and approaches. People will ask questions that challenge the direction. Ideas and solutions may not be clear. This is when you need to step up, set direction, and keep people focused on their next actions. There are crucial (although sometimes uncomfortable) conversations you need to have that will build both organizational and leadership trust and respect.

Acceleration

Once the initiative is announced, you can be tempted to move on to the next business challenge. Don't do this; leading change means staying visible, removing obstacles, and providing support and feedback as your people work in a new way. Leading change starts with acknowledging people as key assets to accelerating results. In Chapter 11, we review ways in which you can easily address the deployment challenges and provide ample positive reinforcement.

CASE IN POINT

A Case for Change Helps Leaders Align Around a Global Strategy

A multi-billion-dollar company had grown through local and regional acquisitions. The company was a key player in select products on a regional basis, but had not done enough to capture the global synergies. The company started to lose market share to two of its competitors, which were building global businesses by aggressively expanding through investments in R&D, marketing, and acquisitions. The strong regional presence that had been a strength was now a significant limitation in the face of globalizing competitors.

Previous attempts to get the regions to work together on a global strategy had failed. While the conversations sounded productive, few actions were actually implemented. The CEO knew that, for a global solution to work, it would need to provide value to the regions. A group of the company's regional leaders and experts was chartered to find points of commonality as the basis of a global strategy aimed at recapturing the company's competitive advantage.

The group's conversations began by sharing local challenges, opportunities, and areas of common interest, and then identifying how to take advantage of their size, regional expertise, and market excellence to create a shared vision. The group mapped out key initiatives to build a global business model, including centers of excellence using a common set of principles. The leaders quickly realized that gaining agreement on action plans would take candid conversations. The leaders shared the challenges in engaging their people in a global approach when the regional benefits perhaps were not clear. To enroll their respective areas, they jointly developed a case for change that would present a compelling vision of a global strategy.

These conversations were different from previous ineffective ones, because the leaders acknowledged their areas of commonality and differentiation to come up with a solution that would maintain local competitive advantages, while transitioning to global consistency. The case for change became the leaders' tool for communicating the compelling vision of the future global approach. Instead of getting bogged down in complexities, they focused on key areas of commonality to get things started.

Key Takeaways from Chapter 3

1. Business plans rarely link the business solution to the actions of an organization's leaders and people. A compelling case for change converts the business plan into information and actions that people can understand, so that they know what to do, why it is important, and what is expected of them.

2. A case for change starts with the current situation, creates a picture of the future, explains why change is necessary, sets out how success will be measured, identifies the actions to attain the future, and tells people what they themselves need to do. Figure 3-1 provides questions to facilitate a discussion about developing a case for change.

3. The five "A-list" keys to leading change are: Accountability, Agreement & Alignment, Acceptance, Actions, and Acceleration. Leaders must understand how these five keys provide a framework for successfully leading change by unlocking the potential of people in the organization. The change will not happen – and the results will not be delivered – unless the leaders attend to these keys.

PART II

Make Change Happen

As I grow older, I pay less attention to what people say.
I just watch what they do.

—Andrew Carnegie

Chapter 4

Develop the Leader Change Roadmap

*Let us not be content to wait and see what
will happen, but give us the determination to make
the right things happen.*

—*Peter Marshall*

Leaders move rapidly to bring innovative products and solutions to market so that they can increase the organization's revenue and return on investment. To lead change initiatives in today's dynamic and complex business environments, a leader change roadmap provides the leadership implementation strategy and structure for leaders to execute the changes. Successful implementation of a change initiative requires a business plan, a case for change, a project plan, and leadership plans all working together. The leader change roadmap brings these pieces into a unified whole.

A Framework for the Leader Change Roadmap

A leader change roadmap is developed through a series of strategic discussions, typically with senior leaders. These discussions create a visual picture or map that integrates the business plan, the case for change, the project plan, and leadership plans that guide a leader's role in the implementation. This roadmap combines the strategy, processes, and people components so that leaders know what to do and see how to engage throughout the implementation. The discussion surfaces challenges and potential sticking points that may need special attention. A leader change roadmap considers the interdependencies of other organizational and day-to-day activities and helps leaders think through and sort, prioritize, and then sequence the actions they need to take to successfully implement one or more strategic initiatives.

Leader Change Roadmap

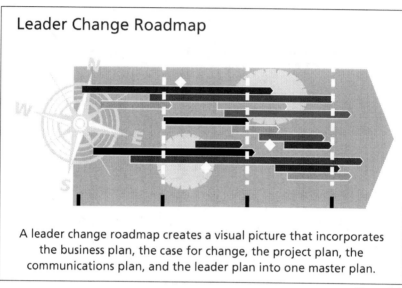

A leader change roadmap creates a visual picture that incorporates the business plan, the case for change, the project plan, the communications plan, and the leader plan into one master plan.

Figure 4-1

The leader change roadmap helps leaders:

◆ Create a compelling vision and sense of direction for others to follow

◆ State the results you and your leadership team will be accountable for

◆ Gain agreement, alignment, and commitment of your leadership team

◆ Meld the business plan, case for change, and project plan into executable leadership actions

◆ Consider the organizational interdependencies and other implications this initiative has on other work aspects

◆ Sort, prioritize, and sequence leadership inputs and activities that may not occur on their own

◆ Give the leadership team clarity about the behaviors required to implement the solution

- Craft a series of consistent, credible, stakeholder-focused communications and messages
- Match your actions with your intentions to reinforce others to take action
- Identify obstacles and issues ahead of time, and plan to remove or resolve them
- Plan how to reinforce the behavioral changes through your coaching and feedback
- Name milestones and small victories to be celebrated on the way to the "new way"

Through the process of developing a leader change roadmap, leaders strategize about how to deploy the initiative and discuss how it fits with the other strategic activities in the organization's ecosystem. In a roadmap session, leaders talk through the trade-offs and implications of the plan. They identify areas of the implementation that need attention and specify how the leaders will contribute to leading results.

By developing your leader change roadmap, you prioritize and sequence the critical actions that will lead to the results you want. Usually there are multiple changes and programs occurring at once. When leaders look at each project separately, they miss opportunities for synergies and fail to spot areas where bottlenecks will occur when people are asked to do two incompatible activities.

If achieving results are important, the actions that lead to the results are crucial components in the execution of strategic initiatives. A leader change roadmap provides the framework to know what to look for and how to be involved to keep your initiative on track. The leader change roadmap aligns the actions at the levels of the individual performer, leader, team, and organization. When you pay attention to establishing the critical few new behaviors and aligning appropriate actions throughout the leadership team, you can accelerate the change initiative. This requires you to identify the leadership behaviors that you and your team will exhibit to support the new behaviors of others.

Change Results by Changing Behavior

A "behavior" is an action carried out by someone. It is an action you can physically see and observe. It is something someone says or does. If we followed a person around, we could see the person perform this action. For example, if a leader has committed to providing positive feedback to at least three people a day, we could observe and even measure the three instances when this leader provided positive feedback.

This sounds very tactical; however, by specifically naming and observing the behavior, we can coach and reinforce a new behavior to form a new set of habits. Most change efforts do not adequately pinpoint the critical behaviors that must occur to achieve the desired result. As a result, people engage in a lot of activity that doesn't lead to the results. The right behaviors drive results. When those behaviors are not consistently performed, the results fail to be achieved. A leader change roadmap helps leaders think through the areas of an initiative where the leadership and performer behaviors need to occur and helps align the series of behaviors from leaders to performers to ensure that the new behaviors are started, reinforced, and sustained.

Behavior Change Is Your Key Work

Often, leaders delegate behavior changes to the training or human resources area. These professionals can start the behavior change actions, yet change requires additional attention and support to take hold and lead to results. Even before you send people to a session to build technical skills, you need to think through how the new behaviors will be cultivated back on the job. We have all heard the saying "use the skill or lose the skill." Your leadership provides ongoing reminders and positive reinforcement and is a significant component in activating new behaviors and then keeping them going.

Leaders need to be prepared to support their organizations when and where needed. They must keep all the moving parts in motion. They may need to help others start a new way of working. They may need to help people navigate the emotional roller coaster that can cause starts and stops in behavior. If leaders don't provide a safe environment in which to implement the change, they can slow down the change process itself. This is why behavior change is your key work.

People need consistent direction and support to stay on course. If they don't hear from their leaders, their actions may become sporadic. Some people will immediately work in the new way while others will not. When a change effort is new and leaders are highly engaged, people may attempt the new behaviors. When leaders' involvement wanes, often the new behaviors start to slip. If the change is important, the actions and messages from the leaders need to continue until the new behaviors take hold. The time it takes for new behaviors to stick depends on the consequence systems that either reinforce or discourage people from "wanting" to engage in the behavior again. There are those behaviors that are naturally reinforcing to people and there are some behaviors people would like to avoid.

You need to play an active role in encouraging people to "want" to take action and not feel like they "have to" do something. If you truly want new results, you must make sure that your actions and behaviors support the change and that the actions and behaviors cascade through your leadership team and the organization. Here are five change leadership behaviors that can have a strong impact and will get you thinking about what you need to do to encourage new behaviors. Incorporate these behaviors as part of your leader change roadmap.

1. **Be visible and active in supporting the change** – Stay engaged and make sure you stay apprised of what is going on. People will need time to ask questions, process the ideas, and seek support. Walk the halls. Reach out and find out how things are progressing. Take five minutes and give your full attention to hear the answer. Check in at different sites and locations. Ask: what's working? what could be improved? how can I help? Listen to the answers.

2. **Communicate, communicate, communicate** – Continue to explain why the initiative is important and how people fit in. People need to hear the same messages many, many times. Every time you communicate and provide updates, act as if this is the first time you are sharing this news. Even if it's the twentieth time, communicate and answer questions. Determine how people will react to the messages. Tailor your messages, as well as the tone, language, and stories you will tell, to what the audience wants to hear instead of to what you want to tell. You will face some resistance, questions, concerns, and inaptitude. Identify what you can do or say that can help move people along.

3. **Demonstrate resilience** – Resilience is the ability to recover from or adjust easily to misfortune or change. Resilience allows us to find creative solutions in difficult situations. It helps us

move through obstacles with ease. Resilience enables us to maintain our energy level and choose how we want to move in and out of the implementation. When we are aware of our actions, our thoughts, and our emotions, we can consciously decide the best course of action.

4. **Remove obstacles** – It's easy to get caught in a spider web of obstacles and challenges, especially with a new initiative. These obstacles can paralyze even the most motivated individuals. Sometimes it seems as if there are so many rules and beliefs that there is simply no way to make the change initiative a success. People need a place to talk about where they are stuck and what they need from the leadership team to get unstuck. Transform the obstacles into opportunities. Break down the problem into smaller components and ask people what they would do to address the obstacles they are facing. By addressing the challenges head on, you can start to move people in the right direction.

5. **Provide positive and constructive feedback** – Positivity feeds on itself, with more positive behavior becoming contagious and leading people forward. So give positive feedback throughout the initiative, especially when you see that people are moving in the right direction. Go beyond the expressions of "Awesome!" or "Thanks, that's great!" to provide very clear, pinpointed feedback on what you saw – and why it matters. Many leaders seem to think they don't need to give positive feedback. However, research has shown that such feedback motivates people and keeps them on course. You can also use positive feedback to overcome negatives.

It's easy to find the faults and problems. It can be harder to find the small positive behaviors that, if reinforced, can move the project ahead. Be on the lookout to find positive actions, even when you feel overwhelmed by all the problems. By focusing on the positive, more positive action will occur.

Go to **www.thetruthaboutchangebook.com** and click on "Free Book Bonuses" to receive the five Change Leadership Behaviors to add to your routine.

CASE IN POINT

The Need for Senior Leadership Involvement

Let's look at an actual case in a revenue generation model. "Susan" is an account manager. The divisional president is implementing a growth strategy. As part of this growth strategy, the organization wants to collect more customer data, to better upsell and cross sell additional products. The sales team (including Susan) has been asked to complete an online Account Report after every client call. Despite the announcements and training program, after a month, Susan has input only 15 percent of her Account Reports. Susan's days are packed with long lists of activities. Her intention to follow the protocols does not bear fruit.

Your first reaction is that Susan may be the problem. However, Susan is one of the top performers, and has shown significant increases in sales over the last six months. Why isn't she submitting these reports? She attended the town hall and was actively engaged in the training sessions. Her manager has even talked to her about the importance of using the new system for growing future revenue.

But merely going to training and being asked to use the system isn't always enough to ensure that the Account Reports will be submitted. Susan does not hear anything regarding submitting the reports; and she does not know what happens to the reports she does submit. It isn't until month's end that Susan hears that the organization has missed its targets. All too often, leaders step in at this stage and tell people to create the reports, but their criticism and negative comments actually shut down the conversation. What should the leadership be doing to reinforce the new actions of Susan and others?

People can see for themselves that the results are off. Telling people to use the form isn't enough to get people to consistently fill out the customer information. Consider what will motivate Susan and her colleagues to enter the Account Reports. Is anyone reading them? Is anyone giving Susan answers to the issues she has reported? What positive feedback is provided to her for completing a report? Has anyone looked to see whether there are problems entering the reports? Susan and others aren't trying to be obstinate. Rather, there is a disconnect between what was asked and what happens in the field.

The key is to recognize that your behavior and engagement in these conversations has an impact, either positive or negative, on others. Knowing this, use the natural laws of human behavior to your advantage in leading change. If you want a new behavior to occur, the fastest way to see the right action is to provide early and frequent positive consequences in the way of positive feedback and other reinforcers. Positive reinforcement may include acknowledging work efforts or resolving problems to make someone's job easier.

Susan did everything that was asked of her. She attended the announcement. She went to training. She attempted to enter information into the system. Yet she heard nothing back. Leaders were only engaged to tell her what was wrong. Her own assessment was that it wasn't worth the effort and she didn't see the value. She made her own decision to work on other things that provided instant results.

When Susan's president and management finally got involved, they found out that the computer system often froze, forcing people to start over entering data. People like Susan couldn't easily access the system in the field, so they waited until they came into the office. Most important, Susan and others didn't see how entering the information could help them grow revenues. She saw the whole initiative as an information black hole, with no value or information coming back to her that she didn't already know about her clients.

When a new behavior is uncomfortable, feels awkward, and doesn't work, the chances of someone like Susan trying the behavior again are slim. Susan may try it a few times but will move on to complete other things. When leaders are available to participate in the process, review and discuss the information, and provide feedback about the behavior, people like Susan can begin to understand why it's so important that they be actively engaged.

Susan's management team finally realized that they needed to be clearer about what actions they wanted people to take. They also needed to make themselves available to observe and address the bottlenecks and problems.

Shaping New Behaviors

Results are based on actions. Your behaviors of listening, answering questions, providing resources, coaching, and removing obstacles are critical components to enabling performance in the new way. If you want new results, plan new actions. If those actions will not develop on their own, you can accelerate them through providing coaching, feedback, and reinforcement. The reinforcement creates motivation and brings out the discretionary effort and accomplishment that you want from your people.

CHANGE LEADERSHIP ACTIONS

- Develop your leader change roadmap.
- Cultivate behavior change to achieve results.
- Set out the sequence and cascade of leadership actions and behaviors for you and your leadership team. Recognize that a leader's actions can either prompt behaviors or reinforce or discourage future behaviors.
- Exhibit leadership change behaviors:
  - Be visible and active in supporting the change.
  - Communicate with the audience, your key constituents, in mind.
  - Demonstrate resilience as you navigate the change.
  - Remove obstacles and impediments.
  - Provide positive and constructive feedback to encourage new actions.

Figure 4-2

The leader change roadmap provides a way for you to systematically step in and out of the change initiative in ways that help you productively attend to the "people side" of change. Without a leader change roadmap, your behaviors could be too sporadic or scattershot to support the implementation. Here are some steps to consider:

Identify the Right Actions and Behaviors

When you are designing your solution (the change initiative to be implemented), identify and map out the new actions and behaviors you will need to see. As you are designing the solution, you will find bottlenecks, areas where people may not be competent, and places where people will need guidance and support. Find the remedies to these problems – by defining the behaviors you need your people to display – and then align your leadership actions to enable and sustain the new behavior.

Assess the Capability to Act

After you have identified what a person or team needs to say or do, you can determine whether they are capable of performing this action. You can determine whether there will be any obstacles or challenges to performing the action. You can also determine whether your people and teams will be motivated to perform the new action without any prompts or reinforcement. Many times, in periods of change, these new behaviors need to be discussed and reinforced.

After you have gained a true understanding of the capabilities that need to be developed, you can then develop programs to prepare leaders and train people on new skills. The leader preparation sessions should include discussions about how to observe, coach, and provide feedback throughout the change. Technical training, while a way to convey information, isn't effective without on-the-job experience and reinforcements that can happen with the support of management. Leaders at all levels can and should play an active role to ensure that people are able to perform the new behaviors.

Motivate Your People

Individuals thrive on positive feedback and reinforcement. Positive feedback can take various forms, depending on the organization, industry, geography, and group. It needs to be specific and pinpointed; a simple "that's great!" is not enough information to prompt a person to continue an action or behavior.

Positive reinforcement is usually missing in change plans, although it is actually an essential part of change leadership. Reinforcement encourages people to continue to perform new behaviors, even when they feel awkward and uncomfortable. Reinforcement comes in many forms, including coaching conversations, feedback, and acknowledging others' efforts. When people are motivated and inspired, they are willing to give more of their discretionary effort. They see the value of persevering in the face of change to deliver the desired results.

Immediate reinforcement helps new behaviors take seed. These actions quickly add up to move an organization in the right direction. That momentum becomes contagious, and even the resisters jump onboard so they will not be left behind. Motivation comes when you, as a leader, are present, observing, providing feedback, removing obstacles, and encouraging your people to work in the new way.

Set the Cascade of Leadership Behavior

To get results quickly, you need to set up a cascade of behaviors that will take your organization through the change. This sequence tells your leadership team and people what needs to be done, and in what order. Without the sequence, people may do what is easiest or fastest for them, regardless of the priorities in the business plan. Your behavior as leader keeps people to the sequence. Additionally, by cascading behaviors, a leader's actions can encourage others to take positive action.

Recognize that Your Leadership Behavior Matters

A change is announced. Maybe people are sent to a session and then attempt the new behaviors. It doesn't work as planned. They ask a coworker. That coworker tried it once, and it didn't work correctly. This coworker discussion results in two individuals electing to do nothing, or to create their own work-around, or to go back to the old ways of working.

You are in a unique position of seeing whether the cascade of behaviors is working or not. Then you can decide how to keep the behaviors you set out in your leader change roadmap on track. Playing an active role in getting these new behaviors started is critical to achieving the desired outcome. The business plan focuses on business actions. But it fails to identify the behaviors you need to display yourself and encourage in others. A combination of both are needed to execute change.

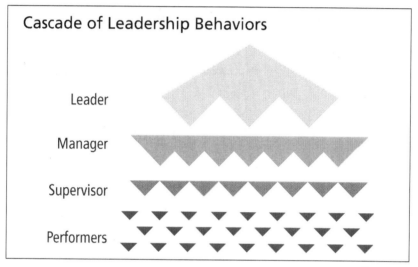

Figure 4-3

In most organizations, there will be certain leaders who don't buy into the change or don't see their role in cascading the messages and actions. Perhaps there are pockets within the organization that simply elect not to engage. This lack of leadership engagement stalls efforts.

Often, one level of leadership gets stuck. Then, it is up to you to engage the leadership team, at all levels, until each member agrees on how to implement the change. You do this by establishing a cascade of behaviors.

Cascade of behaviors. Here is a sample cascade of behaviors that demonstrates the types of actions and behaviors to put into your leader change roadmap:

◆ Name the behaviors in the business plan that may be difficult to implement and maintain. What do you need your people to do or say? Be as specific as possible and name the critical behaviors. Take the time to brainstorm, by role and level, so that you understand what needs to be done. You are likely to find some interdependencies and even some conflicting direction that could impede progress.

◆ Choose the two to three key behaviors that will require special attention. Articulate these behaviors, using action words. Figure out what your people will see as challenges, then develop the appropriate actions and incorporate these actions into the implementation plan.

◆ Identify the level of difficulty (high, medium, or low) to perform these new behaviors. An indication of high difficulty may be that you don't think a person would initiate the behavior simply by being asked to.

◆ Create the leadership behavior cascade. Using the performer behavior as a starting point, determine what leaders at each level need to do and say to support the new behavior. Write out your actions and the actions of the appropriate members of your leadership team to support these new behaviors. What will people need from the leadership team to keep this behavior going? Ensure leadership actions that will reinforce these new behaviors, and make them become habits.

◆ Gather feedback by staying in close contact with your people and leadership team to understand what's working and what can be improved on. Spread positive news and stories about the implementation. Provide progress reports. Ask open-ended questions. Identify and remove obstacles in the way. Inquire how the work going.

♦ Celebrate even the smallest progress. Find reasons to celebrate movement. Also, be honest and realistic with setbacks and use these setbacks as learning opportunities.

When the behavior requests you are seeking do not occur with natural consequences, then it is best to develop the cascade of behaviors from the performer up through the senior leaders. In this way, everyone is aligned and committed to getting the new actions going and accelerating the outcomes.

Key Takeaways from Chapter 4

1. Change requires a business plan, a project plan, and a leadership plan to work together. A leader change roadmap provides the leadership implementation strategy and structure for leaders to execute the changes.

2. The leader change roadmap provides a way for leaders to systematically step in and out of the change process in ways that help them productively attend to the people side of change.

3. The leader change roadmap identifies the behaviors needed from all people throughout the change and provides a way to measure the effectiveness of both the people and the behaviors.

4. Key leadership behaviors in implementing the leader change roadmap include: being visible and supporting the change, communicating throughout, modeling resilience, removing obstacles, and providing positive and constructive feedback.

Chapter 5

Communicate the Case for Change

Just where you are, is the place to start.

—*Pema Chödrön*

You have spent significant time turning your idea into a strategic solution and developing the processes to implement the business plan. Now it is time to get others – your people – involved. Communication starts when you work with your leadership team to create your case for change. It continues when you bring your case for change to your people.

The way to do this is clear: Know what you want to communicate. Communicate the messages in a way that others can process and understand. Be prepared to communicate the same messages over and over. Help management throughout the organization prepare to communicate the same messages. Be prepared to answer a lot of questions, address concerns, and help people understand their parts in the change. Build your communication plan into your leader change roadmap to make sure your communications are supporting the new actions and behaviors you need to see.

Share the Case for Change with Your People

Remember that people need a compelling reason to change. Unlike machines, people will have many questions and will be assessing whether the change is worth their time and energy or whether they can delegate or leave the change up to others.

Communicate the Case for Change

- What is changing?
- Why is it important to make the change?
- Has everyone bought into this change?
- What does success look like?
- What is my role in this change?
- How much will this affect me?
- Will this work lead to the desired result?

Figure 5-1

While you are trying to enroll your people in the solution, your people may simply be trying to understand your messages. These messages need to be clear and succinct, yet still deep enough to help people process the information. One conversation, one memo, or one town hall presentation is usually not enough to handle everyone's questions. People need to take your information and combine it with all other aspects of their work. Too frequently, leaders only think about the change from their perspective, so they miss sharing vital information and scenarios that would assist others through agreement and alignment. The more you can create a complete picture of your desired solution, the easier it is for others to process, understand, and start supporting the change.

Take the time to think through how people at various levels and in different jobs will react to your messages. This will help you build a stronger communication plan covering what people will want to know, where they are heading, and how they will accomplish their work. Use the questions in Figure 5-1 to develop messages and communications that are clear, direct, and informative.

Get the Messages Right

The right communications are key to making sure each level of the organization hears similar, coordinated messages, so that people at all levels are as clear as your leadership team about what they need to do. Coordinated communication starts with preparing leaders at all levels of the organization to deliver the right messages.

Unfortunately, you can get so close to the initiative that when it's time to communicate, you may not feel there is a need for a communication plan. Or, you leave the communications to the human resources or communications departments. These departments do a terrific job of developing the formal announcement presentations and memos and maybe even the initial Frequently-Asked-Questions sheet. Such communications are usually factual, brief, and content-driven, and focus on the "what" for the company. Yet they usually don't address the "how" of leading and implementing the changes.

These formal communications fall short when you want to communicate the next layer of details that your people will need to hear. They tend to say just enough to set the direction for the change. Without the context and more details, the questions your people have will be left unanswered, and the organization will start to create its own explanations, which usually causes unnecessary doubt and uncertainty about the initiative. People need more than the formal communications before they accept the changes and take action.

Big "C"/little "c" Communications

I call the formal communications the Big "C" messages. These broad communications are designed to deliver a generic message to the masses – what is happening and why is it important. Yet these communications don't provide enough detail to engage your people and tell them how to actually carry out the plan.

When only the Big "C" communications are deployed and leaders fail to think through the cascading messages and communications by leaders, managers, and supervisors, it's no surprise that the messages get lost somewhere. If leaders throughout the organization aren't prepared to communicate the same, consistent messages and answer the specific questions, it's very hard to get the organization enrolled and engaged in a plan that involves new actions and behaviors.

Effective change needs little "c" communications, too – the daily, informal communications and interactions between leaders, managers, and the people who perform and carry out the work. It is through these little "c" communications that people figure out what they are supposed to be doing, what results they should be achieving, and how their contributions will be measured. This type of com-

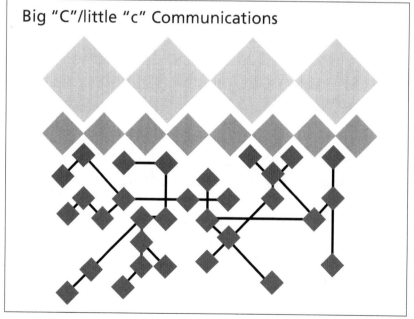

Big "C"/little "c" Communications

Figure 5-2

munications must be prepared by the leaders and management themselves; the human resources and communications departments may help you get the messages started, but they do not have the full context to get them right.

Communications for the Leadership Team

Communications start even before the Big "C" messages are crafted. Communicating the change starts when you work on engaging your leadership team in discussions about the potential solution. You cannot assume that the leadership team will automatically understand your messages and become aligned with the change. More often than not, things are left unsaid. An important inflexion point in creating a successful change initiative is getting your leadership team agreed, aligned, and ready to communicate to the broader organization.

A layer of communication happens when you share information with your leadership team to prepare them for the formal organizational messages. This is the information that starts the cascade of communications throughout the organization. Unfortunately, members of your leadership team may continue to use the formal messages and then get stuck when people start asking questions about what, why, how, and when. Your people will have questions about the physical aspects of the change and, more importantly, individual questions related to their reactions, concerns, and fears. Getting these communications right helps to accelerate people's engagement with the change. Getting them wrong just adds disruption to the organization at a time when people need clarity.

CHANGE LEADERSHIP ACTIONS

- Know what you want to communicate; prepare clear messages.
- Pay attention to the wording and the implications; get your messages right.
- Communicate the messages so people can process and understand them – be prepared to communicate the same messages repeatedly.
- Anticipate the need to answer a lot of questions, address concerns, and help people understand their parts in the change.
- Don't rely only on Big "C" formal communications; your little "c" informal communications are equally important.
- Communicate as frequently as needed to engage your leadership team and your people.

Figure 5-3

Communicate with the Audience in Mind

People will listen to your comments more than to the formal messages. They will pay attention both to what you say and what you *don't* say. They will act according to what they hear and understand. This is why getting your communications and messages right is so important.

I work with one executive who really sweats the details of his communications, right down to the word choice. He knows that the choice of words and tone matter. To help others think and process, he determines how his audience will hear and process the message. He and his team work together on the cascaded messages. They start with what they want to achieve and why it's important. They then take it further to understand the impact the change will have on the leadership team and the people, and they craft messages that address their concerns. The back-and-forth editing process prepares the leadership team to answer sensitive questions. The leaders practice how the communications sound and build in additional messages that will be important to specific people.

I find that many leaders avoid this communications work, and then their leadership team is left to figure it out for themselves. This takes time and often means the leadership team heads off in the wrong direction. It is more effective to work on the communications at the beginning of the initiative. While your leadership team may not be able to address every question in the announcement or presentation, they have the messaging that they can use in their one-on-one and team conversations to help people gain a picture of what's happening, why it so important to address the issue now, and how they can be a part of the solution.

Well-crafted communications help address the physical, mental, and emotional aspects of change. A cascading and consistent layering of the messages reinforces what you need to communicate. Unfortunately, most leaders don't have the time or patience to do this work correctly at the beginning and then find themselves spending more time on the back end, dealing with problems later on.

Disagreement and resistance are normal first reactions. People are absorbing the communications and trying to determine what it all means. They will ask questions for clarification and meaning. They will assess the impact to themselves, to the business, and to others, and will do so at different speeds and levels of comprehension.

Then, in real time, you can observe and respond to problems you cannot ignore. As a leader, you need to stay objective when dealing with your people, making sure they feel they are being heard and that the issues they are encountering are being addressed. This is the best type of little "c" communication.

If the initiative is strategically important to achieving results, there is little room for error. What you and your leaders say and do and how you convey messages are critical to the program. When messages are unclear, people will be less productive and the overall credibility of the initiative will be in question. It's better to take the extra time to properly communicate and socialize the initiative than to be hasty in the delivery of the information.

Enhance the Quality of Discussions

Throughout the implementation, you need to make a conscious effort to increase communication. Communicating the successes as well as the setbacks helps people know where the initiative stands. You can't communicate enough during a change initiative. You almost have to say the same thing over and over until you are exhausted. Then, say the message a few *more* times until you build understanding for what's happening. Each time people hear the message, they are picking up more nuances and details that will help them perform with greater effectiveness.

The quality and consistency of your communications are critical in times of uncertainty. The communications from your leadership team are also critical. Assess how the messages are cascading throughout the organization. All too often, there will be communication gaps, where one layer of leadership is not communicating down to the next. One of the key lessons learned by many leadership teams in mergers and acquisitions is that there is never enough communications. Information often doesn't make its way to the people who need it, and these people often do not have clarity about what is happening and what they need to do to be part of the solution.

Be Aware of Language Barriers

The most powerful type of communication is face-to-face, but this is not always possible in large organizations. Breaking down the language barriers and making sure that the messages are getting through are essential to a right start. Misinterpretation of messages, especially when there are language differences, can hinder the kickoff. Be sure to check and double-check the messages. Make sure that, as messages are translated, the meaning doesn't change. Understand the communication protocols in various business units and geographies, so that people feel like the messages are intended directly for them. An acceptable choice of words in one language can mean something very different in another. Follow up to make sure the messages were received appropriately. This demonstrates endorsement from the top and clears up any misconceptions in the messages.

Key Takeaways from Chapter 5

1. Communication is key for gaining the agreement of your people and making the change happen. The case for change must be communicated to all your people, so that they know why the change is happening, what their roles are, and what results are expected.

2. It is not enough to announce the change and set out the "what" – Big "C" communications. Instead, people need to know the "how" – through little "c", day-to-day interactions and communications.

3. It is crucial to get the communications right, by providing the needed information, answering questions, and listening to your people.

Chapter 6

Monitor and Assess Progress

I have missed more than 9,000 shots in my career. I have lost almost 300 games. On 26 occasions, I have been entrusted to take the game-winning shot – and I missed. I have failed over and over and over again in my life. And that's precisely why I succeed.

—*Michael Jordan*

Leaders often expect and assume that if they have outlined a direction and communicated the approach, the right actions will follow. This is not necessarily true. Yes, it's terrific when change efforts have immediate positive impacts on the business outcomes, but with the normal business complexities and behavioral changes that occur in any implementation, it usually takes longer to see the results.

Some leaders say they are too busy so they leave the tracking of results to the project team and wash their hands of any involvement. This doesn't work. Eventually, the project and consulting teams conclude their work, often before the results are achieved or show signs of being properly maintained. If the change effort is strategic to your business, then *you yourself* must be involved. You are personally responsible and accountable for implementing the change.

You can keep track of the progress of the change initiative through monitoring and assessing. "Monitoring" means using tools, milestones, and benchmarks for determining what is happening. "Assessing" means determining whether the progress is sufficient and, if not, what needs to happen to get the initiative back on track. In reality, monitoring and assessing go hand-in-hand as part of both your project plan and your change roadmap.

Tools for Monitoring

You need ways to take the pulse of the organization to determine if people are implementing the solution. This requires knowing what you want to see (through your business plan and leader change roadmap) and then observing and measuring the actions.

Dashboards and Scorecards

Dashboards and other scorecards are essential tools to provide you with a preview of the business indicators. However, these business results can take months to obtain and don't necessarily provide all the information that leaders need to determine whether the right actions are occurring that lead to business results. By the time the data is collected, the initiative can be way off track. In addition to dashboards, leaders need timely evidence that new behaviors are taking seed and that the changes are progressing on schedule.

Pulse Surveys

Pulse surveys are common ways to check what's happening in the organization and to assess whether messages and actions are getting through. Pulse surveys give quick feedback and can provide opportunities for people to comment. Although the surveys are anonymous, most people can be skeptical of them and so may be reluctant to comment. People need to know they can share comments without repercussions. For these surveys to work, leadership needs to create a safe vehicle for people to express their concerns.

If not, people will tell you what you want to hear, making the usefulness of survey responses plummet.

The use of pulse surveys is one of several ways you can monitor progress. It shouldn't replace the leadership interactions we'll discuss in this chapter. I suggest that you use pulse surveys at key milestones throughout the implementation. Then share the data and take appropriate actions.

Observational Data

Leaders need a way to collect data and assess the progress of the change initiative. The best information comes from different perspectives – the organization, the functions or business teams, and the people. Additionally, it helps to consider the impact of the change on customers or clients. By reviewing progress from different perspectives, leaders can come to understand which adjustments are required to get full engagement.

Pulse surveys and observational data are leading indicators. Such data provides real-time input to what's going on. It goes beyond the project plan milestone completion to include the actions and behaviors in your leader change roadmap.

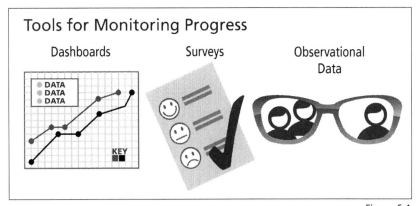

Figure 6-1

Actions for Assessing Progress

When I work with leaders, I suggest that they use the following actions to assess the progress of the change initiative.

Listen and Observe

There is a point where the project team hands over the implementation to the leadership team. Project team members are keen to get back to "real" work. The sooner the project team can hand off the project and declare victory, the sooner the organization can declare victory, or let the project die from neglect. The transition from project team to leadership team is an important inflexion point.

At the point of the handoff (or throughout the early implementation, if you do not have a project team), it is critical for you to listen and observe, so that you can accurately assess where the organization stands in the change process. If you lead a large or virtual organization, you may not have many direct interactions. In such cases, you listen and observe through conference calls, emails, and other forms of communication, and by tracking deliverables. When in doubt about the level of engagement and progress, it is best to get on an airplane and visit people directly. This will save you time and money in the long run.

To ensure that the leadership cascade of behaviors makes it down to your people, use the following questions to determine how engaged and effective your leadership team is in implementing the change effort:

◆ Are leaders facilitating kickoff and launch sessions with their team to communicate the corporate messages?
◆ Are leaders facilitating ongoing implementation discussions with their teams?

- Are leaders surfacing ideas and issues in management team meetings?
- Are leaders meeting one-on-one to discuss the new behaviors with their direct reports?

The actions of your leadership team can provide inspiration and motivation for others. Forums such as town halls, lunch-and-learns, and team meetings are terrific ways to interact with people and discuss aspects of the implementation. You and your team can use every interaction to ask how things are going and find out where people need help. Then you can promptly follow up to keep the energy moving in the right direction.

Follow the Behaviors

You should assume accountability for observing your people's behaviors and providing any feedback, as part of the normal course of business. I've seen companies hand this responsibility off to project teams, but when this happens, there is a tendency for behaviors to be compliant although not sustainable. If you are engaged directly, you can follow how your people are working in the new way and correct actions as needed.

A line item on a project plan can sound pretty simple. When the organization tries to implement that action, the people can struggle with the multitude of new behaviors and handoffs. The project activity may require different functions and business areas to work together. Often there are preexisting dynamics that make it difficult for proper work handoffs to occur. This may require the leadership team to assist in building the collaboration and decision-making across those businesses or functions that are impacted. When leaders directly monitor the progress, they can quickly help the organization connect the actions and rectify any disconnects. As leaders are watching the activities, they should be on the lookout for ways to engage and motivate people to reinforce new behaviors.

Implementation efforts require that you, your leadership team, and your people all be involved. If you want to accelerate results, then observing, assessing, and modifying the behavior changes are important parts of executing the plan. And this work falls to you and your leadership team.

Measure the Engagement of Your Leadership Team

In change initiatives with a goal in mind, everyone needs to be pulling the oars in the same direction to accelerate results. It's easy to convince yourself that you don't have to be involved, because you are working on more important strategic endeavors. Your leadership team, too, may nod their heads in agreement, but not become engaged in the initiative. If you ask them why, they will offer many reasons: "Our group is different." "We're busy implementing other, more strategic initiatives." "We'll get to this when we can."

This "wait and see" passive agreement really means they have no intention to get engaged. They might take some initial actions and participate in the obligatory prep session and announcement. They may even facilitate their team discussion, but then nothing happens. If you follow up with them, they may politely say they are "working on it."

In a change initiative, all levels of leadership need to endorse and communicate the change. If you and your leadership team are not focused on the initiative, progress stalls. Your people see mixed signals, so they do not exert the energy you want. After a few months, the initiative slowly dies and is replaced with the next top priority. People learn that if they wait long enough, they don't need to put in too much effort, and they can move on to the next initiative.

The organization needs to see consistency of leadership engagement so that all parties can recognize that the change is for real. When people see you and your leadership team getting involved, they know it's time for them to get engaged. If the change effort isn't making progress, ask yourself, "Is the leadership truly engaged? What about the leaders at the next level? Where is the disconnect?" With a few simple questions and direct observation, you can quickly determine where the change isn't taking hold. When you have this information, you can get at the root cause of the failure of the initiative.

Make Sure You – as Leader – Stay Engaged

Continue to stay engaged and follow up throughout the implementation. This consistent follow-up helps you assess what is really happening, so you can address problems before they slow your progress. Stay in touch with key influencers and stakeholders, who can decipher and convey messages. Don't be afraid to open up and create dialogue and conversations. Expect to have people ask some tough questions and even object to decisions. It's part of the process of moving toward acceptance and adoption. This process is accelerated through good communication and the sharing of positive gossip and accomplishments.

As you go through the processes of gathering and assessing information, you can take advantage of the opportunities to remind people of the benefits of the change. They can easily get lost in the activity and not see the forest for the trees. People may need reminding of the case for change – and the benefits the change will bring.

Sometimes you will not realize that the initiatives and daily activities you have initiated can be very overwhelming to your people.

Assess the situation and determine if your people need help in focusing and prioritizing. Consider focusing your people on accomplishing just one or two instead of trying to handle ten items and getting nothing accomplished. Be available to address the challenges and remove the obstacles to pave the way to performance.

CHANGE LEADERSHIP ACTIONS

- ◆ Monitoring and assessing progress covers both business activities and the behavior change activities in the leader change roadmap.
- ◆ To assess the progress of behavior change:
  - ▪ Listen and observe.
  - ▪ Follow the behaviors.
  - ▪ Measure the engagement of your leadership team.
  - ▪ Make sure you – as leader – stay engaged.
  - ▪ Monitor new behavior through leadership coaching.
- ◆ Involve the steering committee in assessing progress.

Figure 6-2

CASE IN POINT

Assessing New Behavior through Leadership Coaching

One particular company was experiencing a dip in revenue. Industry data showed that companies like it could increase and expand sales by asking for and gathering specific customer data. The competition was opening locations seemingly on every corner. The company saw an opportunity to expand sales, but without the customer information it was difficult to determine which of the many products and services to target.

During customer interactions, the company's people were expected to ask three questions and input the answers real-time into each customer's profile. The people went to training on how to conduct the interviews and how to input the data into the system. After a while, the leadership team started to review data monthly on customer up-sells and cross sells; they could see that nothing was happening. Only 10 percent of the people were collecting data. Most tried to ask the questions but gave up because customers got annoyed by the questions. When people did get answers, they encountered problems in entering the data: The screens were slow to load and would lock up. Managers didn't ask their people about customer conversations, but focused the monthly team meetings on revenue shortfalls. People began to dread being asked about the customer surveys during executive visits. The president wanted to resurrect the program to create a consistent customer experience. It was important that the entire organization be involved.

A solution was created that engaged leaders and associates in the survey procedures. Clear roles and behaviors were defined, for everyone ranging from executives to customer service people. Leadership kickoff sessions included tips and tools for engaging in coaching conversations. New training emphasized encouraging discussions to enhance the customer experience while asking the three vital questions.

The company made efforts to support the customer service people, acknowledging that negative feedback from customers was demotivating to representatives trying to collect the customer information. The leaders found that debriefing conversations and strategizing about how to handle objections increased survey responses. Monthly one-on-one conversations and team meetings were redesigned to focus on techniques for asking questions and overcoming objections.

Executives, leaders, and the people started to use their time to practice and prepare for customer conversations. At first, it felt very awkward and uncomfortable for all of the company's people to change their behavior, but the leaders continued to reinforce the new behaviors and respond to input from their people.

Within six months, the company was able to institute the survey process throughout the organization and could use the input to drive fresh marketing campaigns. The company learned a valuable lesson about the power of focusing on the behavior of its people and the engagement of all levels of management in implementing strategic solutions.

Involve the Steering Committee

Steering committees often provide oversight and sponsorship to ensure that the implementation is progressing. Sometimes, though, steering committee meetings turn into blaming sessions, with leaders pointing out all the implementation faults and wrong behaviors. Make sure you involve your steering committee in setting out and reinforcing the ways in which the leaders can continue to cascade behaviors and messages and can reinforce the new way of working. Cultivate a feedback-rich environment where people feel comfortable both when sharing the successes and when discussing the obstacles. While monitoring helps focus your people on what matters, you need to make sure your steering committee discussions focus on the good *and* the bad, on the productive as well as on what's *not* working. If your steering committee becomes simply a place for blaming and complaining, people may become detached from the initiative. The steering committee should be part of the solution, not only the critique.

Encourage individual steering committee members to play roles in supporting the change effort. Ideally, the steering committee is instrumental in creating the leader change roadmap and thus endorses and becomes accountable for executing the initiative. Committee members can create forums to communicate messages, gather information, work on removing barriers and obstacles, share positive gossip, and drive the new behaviors throughout the organization.

Key Takeaways from Chapter 6

1. Leaders have many tools for monitoring change: dashboards and scorecards, pulse surveys, and observable data.

2. Assessing progress goes beyond checking off items in the business plan. Sustained change requires behavioral change.

3. Leaders can assess behavioral change by: listening and observing, providing feedback, measuring the engagement of the leadership team, and staying engaged themselves.

4. The steering committee must get involved in the change implementation, so that its members can understand what is happening and can then reinforce productive activity.

Chapter 7

Manage Resistance

You cannot control what happens to you, but you can control your attitude toward what happens to you, and in that, you will be mastering change rather than allowing it to master you.

—*Sri Ram*

People can take business change very personally. The change may affect what they do and how they perform in their role, and possibly even their livelihood. Early in history, change could actually be fatal; we developed a protective instinct that became hardwired in our brain. When this instinct – our fight or flight mechanism – kicks in, we are reminded to take care, to protect ourselves against harm, to be cautious and wary about this new situation. Some people run for cover, express anger or denial, or even blame others. They may need to vocalize their feelings. They need facts and details to see that the change is real. Or they may resist the change.

Why People Resist Change

When individuals hear there will be change, they usually wonder:

- ◆ What's going to happen to me?
- ◆ Is it a big change or a small change?
- ◆ How will this affect my work?
- ◆ Will my efforts be valued?
- ◆ What should I do about the change?
- ◆ Is my job in jeopardy?
- ◆ What's in it for me?
- ◆ Whom can I trust?

People will search for answers. In today's get-it-done-now world, people are expected to quickly shift with the changing direction. People are already on edge, trying to stay on top of the daily work load. When they are asked to change quickly, a frenetic, highly charged sense of urgency plays out in their conversations, emails, phone discussions, and interactions. They crave a safe place where they can assess the situation and gather the facts. They want to be able to look at their options without being labeled as "against" or "resisting" the change. They need an empathetic ear whereby people listen to their concerns and help them make productive choices.

Why People Resist Change

People resist change for many reasons:
- They think change signals loss for them.
- They didn't see the change coming.
- They don't believe the change is necessary or will succeed.
- They weren't involved in the decision.
- They don't see clear outcomes.
- They don't see a compelling enough reason to make the change.
- They don't think this is a great time to launch yet another initiative.
- They think the change may benefit the business, but not them.
- They think everything is fine the way it is.

Figure 7-1

Often, people wait and see what's going to happen before putting forth much effort. Perhaps 10 percent of the people excitedly jump into the work; another 10 percent likely never get on board. The

> ## CHANGE LEADERSHIP ACTIONS
>
> To manage resistances:
>
> ◆ Create a clear case for change.
>
> ◆ Get people talking.
>
> ◆ Understand the specific concerns.
>
> ◆ Share the "What's in it for me?"
>
> ◆ Help people make their own decisions.
>
> ◆ Make people an integral part of the solution.
>
> ◆ Set mutual expectations.
>
> ◆ Coach and provide positive reinforcement early and often.
>
> ◆ Create a trusting environment to make change happen.

Figure 7-2

rest of the people will require direction, guidance, and support to work through and accept the change. If you acknowledge and address the resistance, you may be able to create a "tipping point" for people to get engaged.

Move People from Resistance to Acceptance

If you can bring a semblance of calm to a period of change, you are more likely to achieve the business results you want. You can help create the calm by moving your people to acceptance. This is feasible if you assess your organization and prepare for the resistance you may encounter. If you ignore resistance, hoping that it goes away, you may find that you are creating more disruption and prolonging the transition period.

When you unlock the potential of people by facilitating change conversations, you unleash opportunities to accelerate the change initiative. You do this by assessing where people have concerns and resolving objections ahead of time. While you will not be able to resolve all the objections, tackling some of the critical ones will aid in building credibility around the change effort.

This starts with leaders understanding their own reaction to change and recognizing that each situation may bring different emotions. Only then can leaders recognize that people will need some time to learn, assess, and accept the change. If you can move people from resistance to acceptance, they can be part of achieving the goals.

When resistance is left to fester, people start to exhibit unproductive behaviors. You do not want people to make short-term decisions for personal protection or gain. You certainly do not want personal agendas or the formation of cliques and small factions to inhibit the opportunity to improve the business.

Successful change efforts require strong commitment and engagement by leaders, a commitment that comes from understanding and accepting the change. Identify the key constituents who need your support. Gain agreement and alignment around the case for change. Throughout the implementation process, reinforce key constituents and help them resolve challenges. Provide ongoing communication and progress updates so that people stay engaged. When people know what's in it for them, they see the reason for the change, and can move forward.

If you anticipate that the level of resistance will be exceptionally high, then build into the case for change, the announcement, the business plan, and the leader change roadmap the proper tools and support systems to help people think through, talk through, and move through the change. This may include change-readiness sessions and other support to help people navigate the change. Provide leaders with the tools to lead change, and check in at various phases to ensure that people are engaged.

Create a Clear Case for Change

Create a clear business plan that outlines the future vision. Lay out the case for change, using simple, clear language. Tailor these messages to the audience so that your people can understand the purpose and sense of urgency and can see their role in the change. Giving people a 50-page document to inspire acceptance and action is not realistic. It helps, instead, to use language and a tone that aids people in understanding what's in it for them. A one- or two-page outline containing the right words, metaphors, and visuals can be powerful messages to provide that compelling reason for people to believe this is the right thing to do.

People don't resist change; they resist *being* changed. People don't resist change that they believe will work. People will accept change when they know it's in the organization's and their own best interest. When leaders can enable people to want to change versus trying to change people, leaders can ignite people to action. This requires providing the forums and safe venues for people to talk, ask questions, and work through the change process. This may sound like extra work, but when leaders ignore the resistance to a change, the energy and momentum of the initiative stalls. It takes significant effort to reinvigorate the change, if indeed it can be done.

Get People Talking

People want to be heard. When people don't feel it is safe to talk, they will find forums to express their opinions. So instead of shying away from the change conversations, facilitate these discussions. The use of group forums and one-on-one discussions can provide a safe environment for people to ask questions and process the information. These conversations let you know where people stand. This is the time to listen actively, without judgment. You will learn in the process but do not need to know all the answers; you are listening and allowing people to talk through the change. The point is to help people make the choice to move through their resistance. Building the trust and respect during times of change allows people to move to acceptance.

When people are kept informed, they have a context of why things are occurring. When people hear nothing, they expect bad news. People don't know what to do or where they stand. It helps to take small steps and keep people focused on what they can do, as opposed to what will not work. Bring the hallway chatter into the room and address it head on. Enroll and engage people instead of telling them what to do. Saying, "It's going to be great!" isn't sufficient to get people on board.

Understand the Specific Concerns

Leverage discussions to hear and address the concerns. As much as you can anticipate the challenges, work to resolve these objections ahead of time. Some people will experience loss. Others will express anger that they weren't involved in the decision. There will be others who may not think they have the energy or ability to work in the new way. If you are aware of what people are saying and doing, you can address these concerns and provide inspiration and motivation to try new actions. As the concerns are addressed, people will begin to take part in the effort.

Share the "What's in It for Me?"

A key question on most people's minds will be "How does this impact *me*? What do I do to make sure I do not lose my job?

What's in it for me to put forth the energy to be part of this effort?" It can be difficult for people to move to action when they are still processing how the change affects them. People may be thinking, but not saying, "Is it feasible? What happens if I fail? Where does this initiative fit with everything else I'm doing? How am I going to make this work?" People will assess whether it's safer to proceed or instead to be wary. You can help your people recognize the reasons to believe and be involved in the solution. As you develop the case for change and a leader change roadmap, incorporate actions and messages that help people see "what's in it for them."

Help People Make Their Own Decisions

People like to be in control of their own destiny. It's hard to do that if people feel they don't have all the information or if they feel they are being pushed in a direction they haven't chosen. It's important to give people the forum and opportunity to work through the aspects of the change initiative that affect them. Recognize that high performance comes when people personally choose to be part of the change. The changes you are proposing may not be for everyone; some people may choose to move on to other things. It's better to let people move on gracefully than for you to beg and plead for them to accept something they don't want.

Make People an Integral Part of the Solution

Often the initial decision to make a change is made on behalf of the organization. People can feel as if they aren't given a choice and are not being empowered to make decisions. When leaders can find opportunities to include their people in the process of decision-making, there is a higher likelihood that people will move through the resistance to engagement.

Set Mutual Expectations

To assist people in becoming engaged, let them know what is expected. Help people think through and analyze for themselves what is happening. Be clear about what's known and what still needs to be worked out. Acknowledge whether the transition will be easy or difficult, so that people can set their own expectations. Include in these discussions how people should work together, how often they will hear updates, and what they need to do to be part of the change.

Most people, when given the information and time to process the changes, will make the choice to accept the solution and engage in the actions. A few may not feel this is right for them. In these instances, arrangements can be made for them to move on to something else.

Coach and Provide Positive Reinforcement, Early and Often

When people start to work in the new way, they may need encouragement to keep going. Positive reinforcement is a powerful tool to help people when they feel uncomfortable about making changes. Consistent, positive reinforcement helps accelerate behavior change. Providing ongoing feedback helps people know when they are moving in the right direction and how to take corrective action if they're not.

Too often, people's concerns and questions are shut down. Instead, create a coaching and feedback-rich environment so that people have a safe place to go to ask questions, try out new ideas, and fail fast, so that they can eventually build the competency and motivation to perform in the new way.

Create a Trusting Environment to Make Change Happen

Treat people with respect. In the change process, people will have good days and bad days. People may move through the roller coaster of emotions. This is normal. When we plow right through, we take people off guard and they aren't able to perform at their best. They are constantly defending or on attack. It becomes hard for people to stay clear, focused, and able to act. Give people an opportunity to find their change resiliency. Then they will help you make the change you want to happen.

CASE IN POINT

We Know Better: Regional Resistance to Headquarters Initiatives

In my line of work, I often see people in the business units, regions, or functions resist the organizational changes championed by headquarters, even when the changes are intended to benefit the business. This resistance can overshadow the necessary efforts and progress to deliver results.

One company's systems were so antiquated that its people had to perform significant additional work to compile and use data. This limited the ability of the company to provide products and services to customers. The business units, regions, and functions agreed that a solution was needed, so the company invested in an Enterprise Resource Planning (ERP) solution to automate and streamline the business systems. When it came time to implement the solution, several regions and functions ignored or resisted the change, often in subtle and varied ways. Some regions didn't send regular representatives to project implementation meetings. Others actively attended but didn't follow up on action items. The CEO recognized that the resistances were originating among senior leaders and cascading through the organization as people were directed to handle more pressing matters. The regions and functions saw the new systems as taking away local autonomy or requiring significant input with little benefit. The closer the regions came to the "go live" date, the more that issues and exceptions seemed to come up.

When resistance to change is not identified and resolved, it can hijack a solution. The CEO realized that it wasn't enough to outline the merits of a new system; he needed to make sure his leaders agreed to the solution and were willing to accept and implement the changes. As part of the implementation process, the CEO and his leadership team discussed the implementation challenges and regional resistances, to come up with a concise list of "must-do actions" to build acceptance and unlock the implementation. At first, the leaders were apprehensive about discussing the challenges, but they quickly found common ground and ways to help people move into action.

Key Takeaways from Chapter 7

1. People resist change for many reasons, especially when they see the change as loss, don't think the change is necessary, and can't see the benefits of the change for themselves.

2. Leaders must move people from resistance to acceptance in order to gain cooperation and induce performance for the change initiative to succeed.

3. Leaders can manage resistance by setting a clear vision of the future, getting people talking, addressing specific concerns, helping people understand what the change means for them, making people part of the solution, setting mutual expectations, and providing positive reinforcement.

4. Leaders must be aware that the more complex the organization, the more locations in which resistances can arise. It is necessary to identify and resolve resistances in all regions, functions, and business units for change to be fully implemented.

Chapter 8

Lead During Complexity

A pessimist sees the difficulty in every opportunity;
an optimist sees the opportunity in every difficulty.
—Winston Churchill

Leaders often find themselves required to push through significant change to keep up with their marketplaces. What grew the business last year may not be relevant in the next. The work of change is never complete. With change comes a level of complexity and ambiguity that can be overwhelming and that must be addressed throughout the change initiative.

Change seems to come in waves. A new strategy is set in motion, which triggers new processes, which triggers a new structure, which in turn creates new roles and responsibilities, and on and on. Frequently, there are numerous change initiatives happening simultaneously. Each initiative is focused on a different aspect of the business. One initiative starts before the previous one has had a chance to demonstrate its results. A new round of initiatives launches from one business cycle to the next. Some initiatives are scrapped mid-implementation in favor of the next surefire solution. If the business isn't meeting its targets, you can expect to see further initiatives aimed at solving the problem.

To those looking on, it seems as if the leaders throw a bunch of ideas at the white board to see what sticks. If one initiative isn't working, they move on to the next. Add to this a revolving door of new leaders: Every year or so, new leaders step in to make things happen. With big agendas and visions, another round of initiatives gets under way. If people wait long enough, they think, the next leader will transition out before the current slate of initiatives has been implemented. Change on top of change on top of change makes people exhausted and wary. They take a wait-and-see approach to figure out where things are headed before putting too much energy into an initiative. Part of leading change is helping people navigate the many initiatives. This means being willing to lead the organization through these complexities.

Organizational Complexity

Different vantage points throughout an organization provide differing views of a change initiative. When leaders understand the impact of change from the organizational, group, and people levels, they can use this information to remove complexities and accelerate the change. In Chapter 2, we started the discussion about how to understand and assess the changes from the perspectives of the people, the teams, and the organization. Let's take a deeper look now at these different perspectives and ways to reduce complexity by managing the collective perspective.

Organization Level

When you are at the top of an organization, you have the benefit of looking at the entire ecosystem. You make decisions and set out initiatives that others will be reacting to and implementing. This 30,000-foot view allows you to observe the migration from the old way to the new way and provides a look at how your overall assumptions are playing out. While you may not have the detailed perspective of each business unit or function, you can easily compare and contrast how the various groups are embracing or rejecting the change. You have an advantage in being able to spot issues and disconnects across businesses or functions. At the organization level, you can determine whether the change will move you toward your goals. You have a wide-angle and broad view, but you must remember that you may not be seeing the reactions to the change that will be arising and visible at the group and person levels.

Communication from the organization level focuses people on the overall future vision, provides a visual roadmap of how to navigate the way forward, and sets out guiding principles for people to get involved. Messages are specific to the organization, but leaders tend to rely more on the Big "C" communications, and not enough on the little "c" ones that can engage people individually (as we discussed in Chapter 5).

Group Level

Groups have additional clarity beyond the enterprise view around how the change will work and where the change creates problems for them. Groups also have an experience with prior changes and are aware of what didn't work the last time. At the group level, cultural dynamics, agendas, and politics can cause difficulties if not addressed early. Most initiatives will modify the ways of working; this will cause some people to oppose this change, as they may well feel some loss of control and influence.

Because business units or functional areas see the change from their own perspectives, they can develop clearer assumptions and plans that can positively affect the group's ability to execute the change. People start to rally around specific actions. A group can also get insular and stuck in a silo if it doesn't reach out and work with other groups. Then the handoff of work from group to group becomes clunky and disjointed.

At the group level, the messages and direction can be quite specific. Use specific examples and stories to help make the change relevant to the group in particular. Does the group need to delve more into the strategy or the facts? Does the group need more time to process how the change will work? Maybe the group needs a deeper discussion about the impact the change has on its people, customers, or other key stakeholders.

Communication at the group level may simply echo that from the organization, unless the group's leaders take steps to make the messages specific to the group. If designed properly, these cascaded group discussions can delve into more details, help clarify the change, and begin to enroll and engage the group to action. At the group level, plans are more specific than at the organization level. Despite the additional level of detail, some leaders may find it challenging to engage individual workers. There is true value in looking at any change initiative from the various perspectives to build the right plans.

People Level

The people level addresses the concerns and actions of individual workers. What, specifically, are the people thinking, feeling, and doing? What do they need to process to understand the change? How can you help each individual worker accept the change? What do you need to do or say that may help them adopt the change?

At the people level, you can develop specific plans to help individuals take action. You may provide training, job aids, and other information to help them do their work. At the same time, you need to engage in listening, observing, and providing feedback to reinforce the learning and associated behavioral changes. With practice, repetition, and the appropriate reinforcement, the new behaviors can start to take hold to form new work habits.

Reduce Organizational Complexities

As you can see, decisions and approaches can shift drastically when looking at change from the various vantage points. You need to look at and be able to lead change from these different perspectives. Some of the things to watch out for are the following:

- **Us vs. Them Mentality** – You may have experienced creative tensions that often arise between headquarters and the business functions. Maybe headquarters charters a strategy but takes a "we know best" approach, without acknowledging or addressing the business implications. Or the business unit may elect to ignore headquarters' instructions, believing *it* knows better. While some creative tension can yield better solutions, it can create barriers and interfere with achieving results. It can be helpful to consider various perspectives ahead of deploying the solution. Headquarters, business units, and functions all need to work together to find the right solutions.

- **Tensions between Business Units and Functions** – Business units and functions are created as needed to do certain work. Each has its own identity and culture, which can lead to cross-organizational differences. When a global initiative is rolled out, leaders should make sure that the business and functional differences aren't interfering with the flow of business. To make global deployments successful, leaders need to remove any misunderstandings and find common ground.

- **Lack of Role Clarity** – Most people prefer to make their own decisions. When you are part of an organization, this isn't always feasible. Successful implementations clearly define roles and responsibilities, so there are no misconceptions about who makes which decisions. If roles are not clear, people may think they are empowered to make their own decisions. This confusion arises when leaders look at a change from only one perspective and forget that there may be other interpretations of the change.

◆ **It's Their Job** – When the organization treats people like a number or a "widget," people may not exert sufficient effort to solidify change. Deployment strategies need to take into account the impact of a new set of actions on the daily workload, or else important tasks may slip. Understanding the organizational complexities across all levels – from the individual performer up through the leadership ranks – is critical to the success of the initiative.

Leaders who are able to work across the organization are able to successfully execute change. When companies have too much tension and conflict and spend too much energy negotiating among units, they will likely miss opportunities to create lasting business results. It may seem as if too much time is spent gaining agreement and alignment, yet doing this work will actually create the possibility of accelerating change. The strategic discussions and thinking that can occur within an executive team as it builds its leader change roadmap can help reduce the complexities of working across an organization. Chapter 1 discusses ways to prepare to lead change.

Multiple Business Levers of Change

If you launch a new strategy, you will affect the entire business ecosystem. Think of each of the various components of the business as levers. The business levers each serve a purpose and are interrelated. When you adjust one business lever, you need to adjust many others to keep the business working well.

In *The Executive Transition Playbook*, I shared how to create a learning plan using a business ecosystem model, as outlined in

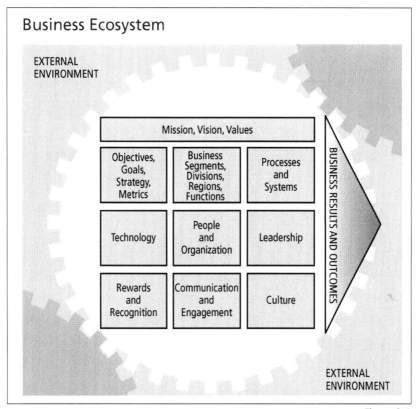

Figure 8-1

Figure 8-1. In leading change efforts, it's critical for leaders to understand how an adjustment of one business lever affects another. For instance, to grow the top line, you implement a new growth strategy and decide to enter a new market. You may need to change core processes to enable the strategy. You may need to realign the organization and adjust work patterns. You may not have the power or ability to control all the areas that need to be adjusted in the scope of the change. You may need to engage other leaders. You may find it easier to focus on the one key lever – say, a growth strategy – than to address the implications for all the business levers, until an issue arises. This single focus may create bottlenecks lower in the organization. People scramble to address the issues, and the temporary fixes may not be sufficient to sustain long-term change.

Before pulling the trigger on the launch of a new initiative, assess the impact that the new initiative has on the other business levers in your organization. Understanding the implications of the change on the entire business ecosystem enables you to make better implementation choices and catch issues earlier in the process.

Leadership Actions

Leading one change effort has its complexities. Layer on the many projects launched from the organizational, group, and functional levels, and things will get complicated in a hurry. Some initiatives complement one another, while others compete for the same resources, meanwhile communicating conflicting messages and direction. Each project team seems to have its own approach to implementation. Some efforts feel demanding and dictatorial, while others work to enroll and engage associates in jointly creating the solution. Some projects start with a frenzy of activity but seem to have no substance or focus. Your people don't know what to expect or how to react.

From your vantage point, you can look across the organization and be able to spot the potential challenges and conflicts. Your task is to strategize and sequence all the moving parts so that the combined initiatives can work toward a set of common goals.

If this change seems complicated for you to manage, imagine what is being asked of your people. One strategic initiative can generate thousands of individual activities in the organization. People need clarity, simplicity, and direction. They need to understand the vision and how all the moving parts fit together, so that they can make the right strategic choices in how they approach all those activities. Otherwise, people will spend too much time on the activities and not pay attention to overall goals. They will gravitate to some projects and abandon others, failing to see that these initiatives could make a substantial improvement for the organization. If you don't provide the structure for how everything fits together into the vision, people may create their own priorities. You need a way to handle the complexities, so that your direction, communications, and action move the organization closer to the overall goal. Let's discuss what you can do to help reduce the complexity and create clarity so that both your associates *and* you can get your arms around the many moving parts.

Simplify, Don't Complicate

Prioritize. Most businesses have long lists of projects. When asked to prioritize, they may pare down the list, but they have a hard time keeping some priorities from creeping back in. Less is more. If there are too many initiatives, the list gets confusing, hard to remember, and overwhelming. You are better off identifying the one to three key priorities and getting started than trying to juggle a long list of projects. People struggle to know what's really important. The most strategically important priorities can get lost with all the other activities. Trying to focus on too many initiatives creates a mess that is hard to lead, will be difficult to execute, and surely will miss the goals.

Simplify. I often hear leaders say there is so much going on that they don't have the time to perform at their best. You may pride yourself on being a multitasker, but are you really bringing your best? Can you listen to the conference call while you are checking email? Are you able to contribute if you are half-listening? You might be able to regurgitate what was said, but can you really process it and make good decisions? You may think you're being highly effective, but you're not. You lose the ability to assess and understand.

Initiatives add new activities to already full schedules. New tasks take longer and, without clear guidance, can absorb a lot of time. Without clear instruction, people need to spend time figuring out what to do and what they no longer need to handle. It's best to simplify the change initiative into concrete actions. Strip away any non-value-added activities and identify work that is no longer needed. The continual removal of unneeded work builds goodwill throughout an organization and frees up resources and possibilities to focus on new priorities. This type of simplification increases the likelihood that your plans will actually lead to the results you want.

Focus. To be an agent of change, you need the dedication and focus to see the journey from beginning to end. When you have many priorities, it can be very hard to focus your energies. Your time and attention gets split and outcomes can be suboptimal. What you focus on will get attention. Without a focus, your work lacks clarity. If you want better outcomes, focus your messages and communicate in a way that is clear and easy to follow.

When the activities in a change initiative seem too complex, break them down into smaller discrete activities, so that your people can see milestones. If your people get discouraged or distracted, help them focus by charting out simple actions and setting realistic, short-term timelines. Encourage people to focus on a particular part of an initiative instead of jumping to other activities that may seem easier to handle.

Find Ways to Inspire Others

You can generate high-level results when your people are engaged and motivated. People *want* to be inspired. However, when they get to work, the demands and the deadlines can drain the life out of them. Over time, they may get numb to all that is happening around them. As a change leader, you need to wake people up, excite them, and help them see that this change will be different.

People look to leaders for inspiration. They look to leaders who can present a bright golden vision of opportunity and hope. They look to those who lead and serve, who don't take them for granted, who bring out the best in them. They look for leaders who will listen and help break down the barriers of complexity so that the complicated becomes simple and attainable.

Are you this leader? This type of leadership starts with the ability to create your own opportunities, to see the world as abundant in

CHANGE LEADERSHIP ACTIONS

- ◆ Understand and address the degree of complexity throughout your organization, down to the individual level.
- ◆ Enhance cross-organizational collaboration to reduce complexities.
- ◆ Be aware of the impact one change effort has on the other business levers in the business ecosystem.
- ◆ Simplify as much as possible by focusing and prioritizing.
- ◆ Find ways to inspire others.
- ◆ Use presence and mindfulness to gain clarity.

Figure 8-2

solutions, and to be willing, even when the chips are down, to provide others with some hope and inspiration. It's less about all the activity and more about spending time observing, listening, and asking others what they think should happen next. It's about getting others involved and willing to bring energy and good work to the journey forward. It's about taking the time to understand others' needs in the context of the business changes and to create the bridge for people to want to be a part of the change.

Use Presence and Mindfulness to Gain Clarity

Change requires that people work hand-in-hand to tackle challenging problems. You cannot afford to miss connecting and working with your people. If you are distracted, annoyed, frustrated, stressed, or busy with other things, you forgo the opportunity to connect with the people who matter.

How can presence help you make better connections and build relationships with your people? Being present means having an awareness of what's going on. From this awareness, you can use internal strength and power to provide direction and guidance. When you are aware, you can choose to listen to the person right in front of you. You can hear and absorb what's actually being said. When you are present, you can decide to listen without judgment, observe the verbal and nonverbal cues, and tailor your responses to meet the needs of others. In this way, you build the credibility and trust to help people navigate the complexities of change initiatives.

When I work with leaders, I often ask, "How do you want to show up? What is your intention? What impact do you want your actions to have on others?" Being aware of what you want to accomplish and how you want to approach the situation is the beginning of preparing to be present. When you take the time to think consciously about your approach, you think and strategize before you step into action together. You are in the present moment.

When you are present and engaged, when you are aware of how you are acting, you can observe how your behaviors affect the actions of your people. Through awareness, you start to make better choices about how to lead. You can prioritize and do your most important tasks.

Mindfulness means you're in the present moment, not worrying about what just happened or what will happen in the future. You're seeing the present situation for what it is without judgment as it unfolds. This reality can be hard to watch, hard to acknowledge and accept. It may mean realizing that a project is really off target. It may mean that people are not in agreement or fully engaged in a solution. Being mindful allows us to determine what to do and how to respond. We can be available and look for opportunities.

CASE IN POINT

Prioritizing, Aligning, and Sequencing Organizational Complexities

A strategy may sound simple until you take a closer look. The strategy may have three to five key imperatives, or pillars. Each strategic pillar may contain multiple programs and initiatives, which have cross-organizational implications. For instance, a strategy could have four key pillars each of which could contain three or more initiatives. This equates to at least twelve initiatives. Managing all the initiatives can become complicated for those implementing the strategy. What are the priorities and how will these initiatives be deployed? If each initiative is carried out in a silo, there will eventually be bottlenecks.

Project and change teams do their best to identify these issues early. However, leaders can play an active role in coordinating across initiatives, so that the work gets done efficiently.

Whether you are a small organization where people wear multiple hats or a large organization with many people doing different activities, you are bound to find challenges in multilayered implementation plans. Each plan has its own issues, given the complexities of organizational change. Sometimes leaders ignore or fail to see the complexities the plans create throughout the organization as people start to carry out the work. Leaders can support these efforts by mapping out the work that needs to be completed along with the routine activities. When people do not get this guidance, the complexities can be overwhelming and resistances are bound to happen.

A particular business was mandated to meet new compliance regulations right when it acquired one of its competitors. So, the organization named a compliance steering committee, a project management officer, and a change management team to oversee the ten work-streams to create a global compliance strategy, a new organizational structure, core work processes, systems upgrades, and product enhancements. A separate integration team was also established for the acquisition. Consulting teams were engaged to support various work components. All these initiatives generated significant activities and requests, in addition to the business and functional work already under way.

Senior leaders knew the importance of being change advocates who could cut through the complexities and interdependencies, so that the direction and action plans given to the organization were specific and clear. The leader change roadmap looked at all the initiatives to show the leaders their role in implementing a global compliance solution while integrating their competitor. As information presented itself, the leadership team could shift and reprioritize the actions in the field. The consistency of addressing the complexities as a leadership team helped to cascade decisions and avoid the confusion of multiple priorities.

Key Takeaways from Chapter 8

1. Organizational change has many moving parts, which adds complexity to implementing the change initiative.

2. One form of complexity involves managing the change from different perspectives: at the organizational, team, and individual levels.

3. Another form of complexity involves the multiple business levers – the parts of the business ecosystem. It is easy to focus on one lever, without understanding or accommodating the changes in the other levers. Successful change addresses the impacts that one business lever has on the entire business ecosystem as all elements strive to develop an integrated solution.

4. Leaders can reduce the effects of complexity by simplifying, prioritizing, focusing, and inspiring others.

5. Leaders, when mindful and present, are able to listen to different perspectives and make decisions amid the complexities.

PART III

Maintain the Change

Your beliefs become your thoughts; your thoughts become your words; your words become your actions…your actions become your destiny.
— *Mahatma Gandhi*

Chapter 9

Measure Progress and Results

If you can't measure it, you can't prove it.

—*Peter Drucker*

Many ingredients are needed to create success: hard work, skill, practice, resources, and a bit of luck, to name just a few. You need a strategy, a plan, and measurements to chart the course and know where you are. You need to use the feedback from your actions, mistakes, and failures to drive your organization toward its goals.

When you measure progress and results, you and everyone involved in the change initiative can stay on top of the goals, know what was agreed to, and assess where things stand. With this information and knowledge, everyone can execute on the work to achieve the results.

Unfortunately, some leaders use measurements only when they see actions and plans failing. They use the measurements to punish people, instead of encouraging, teaching, and getting them back on track. If people see measurement solely as punishment, they will not work with you to collect the data you need and use it productively. If you wait for the end of your initiative to assess the result, you may be too late to reward or correct behavior – and may not achieve what you want.

This chapter explores ways in which leaders can use measurement to lead change throughout the initiative. How you use measurement to enable and reinforce business change becomes critical to how your people accept and adopt the change plans and take appropriate action. Measurements can be valuable guides to assess progress and give feedback as your people work on the change initiative.

Use Measurement to Work Toward and Sustain Change

When you created your business plan and your leader change roadmap, you decided which measurements (both qualitative and quantitative) to use to assess progress, and you built them right into the work plans. Let's review what you should be looking at in terms of the measurements you incorporate into your daily conversations that drive and sustain the change initiative (see Figure 9-1).

Measurement Considerations

- ◆ Which leading indicators are you measuring?
- ◆ Are the measurements a realistic representation of progress toward the goals?
- ◆ Who is involved in the measurements?
- ◆ How do your milestones translate into short-term goals for people to use to monitor their own progress?
- ◆ How will you use the measurements?
- ◆ How will you collect and measure your people's measurements?
- ◆ What is the data telling you?
- ◆ Do you need to adjust the measurements to match the goals and milestones?

Figure 9-1

We've all heard the expression "What gets measured gets done." This means that what we measure is what people are more likely to pay attention to and act on. The measurements give you the data you need to make the right decisions and to revise your plans as needed to improve results. It means that you have the information to inspire, encourage, and facilitate good decision-making.

Build a Measurement Culture to Drive Behavior

If you want an environment that cultivates learning and growth, then approach discussions about how data and measurement drive the desired behavior. In many business cultures, people shy away from the data. Measurement becomes a month-end or quarter-end scramble when business targets are not being met. Too often, measurement discussions amount to a look-back and postmortem about all that isn't working, and little is shared to help reinforce go-forward plans. However, when data is used to positively shape the way people should do their jobs, then individuals, teams, and the organization itself can be proactive in finding the right solutions. So, make measurement a positive influence on actions, instead of a punishment that people will avoid discussing.

You need to play an active role in how measurements are used in your organization. If you weave the use of measurements into the implementation through daily assessment, conversations, and communications, your people can use this information to move from the current state to the future vision. Sometimes the early measurements are more anecdotal and qualitative. These measurement indicators are important, because they are signs that the right actions are occurring.

Measurements can be a terrific learning and reinforcement tool. People are more apt to self-report and use data if they realize that the information contained in measurements will be used to help them solve problems. Understanding what's driving the measurements enables leaders to explore options and find solutions. The measurements themselves can aid in identifying problems or avoiding stumbling blocks that may get in the way.

When I work with leaders, I recommend that they create simple, self-reporting scorecards for people to use to collect individual behavioral information about their progress. For example, if you break behaviors into discrete actions, you can count the number of times you give feedback or how often you listen without interrupting. This practice of collecting, analyzing, and adjusting actions works to build consistency and fluency toward the goal of high performance. Some of the simplest leadership behaviors, like this, can have the most profound impacts on the organization. Measuring actions creates a business culture, where people are focused on progress, actions, and results.

Set Realistic Targets

Goals and measurements should be active parts of the business plan. Realistic goals create targets to motivate people to do their best work. If goals are unrealistic – impossible to attain – people feel defeated even before they get started. Measurement becomes a demotivator. Then the business plan and measurements lose credibility from the start.

When you set realistic goals that can stretch but not fracture an organization, the change effort becomes highly credible. Still, be realistic in setting both goals and timelines. Project plans usually underestimate the time it takes to implement key tasks. People can feel overly pressured when aggressive delivery dates slip.

Efforts lose their energy as people are constantly playing catch-up. Subject matter experts can provide a good read on how the goals and time frame will affect their areas. With such input and agreement, you can assess the interdependencies and reach a mutual understanding of what needs to be done.

Cascade Measurements to Stay Focused on Your Goals

Most change efforts set financial goals and targets that are communicated in the business plan and case for change. The ownership of such financial results usually sits at the highest level of the organization. If you only look at the financial results – those absolute numbers – you miss the opportunity to effect change throughout the organization by using a set of appropriate measurements. If the goals of the initiative seem very distant from the actual work and not related to the changes in behaviors they must make personally, your people may not feel as if they are accountable for any results in the initiative. People need to see how their daily work helps effect the change. The key is to instill measurements at all levels, from the top leader to the full leadership team to the individual workers, so that everyone can be held accountable for their actions, contributions, and outcomes.

Many organizations know what they want key stakeholder groups to do, and may even measure the outcomes after the fact. However, tracking the specific behaviors as they occur seldom happens; nor do organizations identify and track the specific leadership behaviors that will encourage and reinforce the new behavior of individual performers. When leaders and individual performers are clear on what to do and say, they can accelerate the change. The data allows leaders to quickly see what actions are leading to the right results and where things are going off course. With this data, leaders can coach and guide their people during the change process. Behavioral leadership metrics, such as the number of coaching conversations, the number of times a leader provides positive feedback, and the effectiveness of communications, can be key indicators that link the performance of the people to the overall results.

Determine the cascade of leadership and people behaviors and associated measurements that align to the change initiative. The input you get from the measurements will enable you to quickly see if the right behaviors are leading to the intended results. Start with knowing what you want to achieve. What actions do you need to see from your people to know you are on track? What actions do you need to take to enable the actions of your people? What measurements can you develop to track behavior and results down to the individual worker?

Help your people own their actions and be part of the change effort by converting and cascading organizational targets to tangible measurements that can be self-managed and self-reported. Cascade measurement throughout the organization. And remember to add the measurements and actions to your leader change roadmap.

Shape Adoption and Action

If your people do not fully adopt the change initiative and align themselves with it, you will not get the full benefits you want. Let's say you achieve 75 percent of the results with only 25 percent adoption. What results could you achieve with full adoption of the initiative? Measuring change throughout the organization lets you quickly know the areas where you aren't getting full adoption of the initiative.

A divisional president initiated a new, five-pillar strategy. The goal was to expand the revenue base by significantly adding new clients.

An innovative business development process was rolled out to provide account representatives with a host of new business development tools and techniques. In the spirit of "what gets measured gets done," the account representatives were asked to input three weekly actions into their sales system. The goal was to uncover opportunities to grow new business. Management realized that it would need the support of the entire organization to reach this goal.

At first, only a small percentage of account representatives proactively input their actions. Generally, they were not pleased that "Big Brother" would be watching over them. To encourage data input, managers scheduled both monthly one-on-one conversations and team meetings to discuss the application of the tools and prepare for key customer meetings. The organization went from reacting to customer requests to being much more proactive. By getting ahead of the sales process, the organization started to see an uptick in client engagements.

While the program initially was focused on providing new sales techniques, the leadership team's engagement in coaching and supporting account representatives opened the door for other conversations. At first, measuring weekly actions wasn't comfortable. Through consistent reinforcement by leadership on adopting the new way, people quickly saw how the preparation improved their discussions with customers.

Success comes from driving measurement throughout the organization and getting leaders, managers, and people involved in measuring the changes. A cascade of organization goals, defined by different functions, business units, and people, enables everyone to see how their work affects the change initiative.

CHANGE LEADERSHIP ACTIONS

- Decide what you will measure, and build a measurement system you use during and after the implementation to initiate and maintain the change.
- Cultivate a measurement culture to drive behavior.
  - Set realistic targets.
  - Cascade measurements to stay focused on your goals.
  - Shape adoption and action.
  - Create transparency.
  - Capture lessons learned.
  - Stay in the game longer than you planned.
  - Celebrate small wins.
  - Fail fast and move on.
  - Capture lessons learned.

Figure 9-2

Create Transparency

Measuring and tracking can feel time consuming, unless your people can see the value of using the measurements. Be clear about what information you will be collecting and how it will be used. Ask people to be involved in reporting and analyzing their own results. People make better choices and become engaged when they feel they can control what happens to information about their work. If they think their managers are looking over their shoulders and monitoring their actions, they may be apprehensive to participate. Through communication, you can create the transparency that helps your people become comfortable with the measurement process.

Self-Reporting to Create Adoption of New Behaviors

During a merger, a large manufacturing company became concerned that the many integration programs in play would be a significant distraction to employees and contractors. Safety was a top concern, and the senior leader realized that, with all the distractions of the merger, the daily safety talks were likely forgotten during shifts, with the people under pressure to complete the work. The leader knew that whenever new procedures are implemented, people can lose their focus on safety. He needed to find a way to keep safety and reliability at the top of his people's minds, while new procedures and actions were being put into place. He adopted a self-reporting personal safety and reliability scorecard to keep safety protocols top of mind. Everyone in the organization – leadership team, management, and people – carried personal pocket scorecards to track safety procedures and report personal variances. The scorecard measurements were designed to catch problems before there was a major incident.

Any safety variances were discussed in coaching conversations between the managers and the people. These conversations were used as learning opportunities, not as punishment. The key was to encourage self-reporting of variances and create dialogues to help reinforce the importance of safety. The one-on-one conversations and group discussions were aimed at educating and reinforcing safety procedures.

At first, the people were afraid to report variances. When they saw that managers were there to reinforce safety procedures, though, the people became willing to step forward and talk about some of the variances. The daily safety talks transitioned from "telling" people about safety procedures to "sharing" experiences and tips for staying safe. When managers walked through the plant, the people proactively talked with them about safety improvements. As a result, both safety measurements and work productivity improved. The transparency created by the use of personal scorecards created the opportunity for productivity improvements. The managers went from being feared to being seen as supporting and leading the change initiatives.

Stay in the Game Longer than You Planned

Behavior change can take quite a bit longer than you might anticipate. You need to stay involved and help focus people on small, short-term actions to shape new behaviors toward gaining fluency. Until your people develop a level of fluency and the accountability for turning the new behaviors into sustainable results, your role is to guide and support the changes. The use of both quantitative and qualitative information can help you facilitate these conversations. Continue to use this data until the results can be sustained.

Celebrate Small Wins

The uncertainty that always arises during change can make it difficult for people to keep their eyes on the entire initiative. There is a tendency to wait to see some strong, tangible evidence that the results are occurring. Why wait for the results, though? Many actions need to happen before you start to see a glimmer of the results. During the leader change roadmap discussions, identify short-term goals and small wins. Create mini-celebrations to keep people engaged and focused on the small changes that are steadily happening and accumulating. Small celebrations reinforce the desired actions you want to see. They give people clarity and something realistic and tangible on which to focus their attention. Many small successes lead to high performance. Smaller tasks provide more opportunities for reinforcement. That reinforcement can be what keeps your people moving ahead, especially through difficult situations.

Fail Fast and Move On

You cannot expect your people to perform new tasks perfectly, especially if there is no room for error. People "play it safe" and minimize creative solutions when they are afraid to fail. Consider giving your people opportunities to experiment, try new approaches, and use their creativity to develop viable solutions. The idea of embracing failing fast, then finding ways for people to try a new approach, can be very powerful in coming up with innovative solutions. This means that you need to build time into the implementation to try out new concepts. Create a learning environment in which people become comfortable practicing and learning for themselves. This helps your people look at a problem from all angles and identify the best road forward.

Capture Lessons Learned

As your initiative reaches completion, you and your people may want to move on quickly. Do not be too hasty to move on without capturing the many lessons and new ideas you learned along the way that could help the next initiative. Reflect on what worked and what could be improved. Be honest about how leadership and the organization worked together. Figure 9-3 provides a set of questions to use in a debriefing session. Your organization will benefit if you take the time to reflect on and capture lessons learned.

Questions for Capturing Lessons Learned

- What were the success drivers? What are you proud of?
- Whom do you need to acknowledge?
- What could have been improved?
- How will you capture the information in an executive summary?
- Can you create a visual of this initiative from beginning to end that identifies key tools and techniques that you will use in the future?
- How did your leadership communications help or hinder your success?
- How would you describe leadership engagements? What worked? What would you do next time?
- How did resources help or hinder your progress?
- What will you do in setting up the next initiative?
- How will you package your findings so that you can use these insights next time?
- Who would find this information valuable for their next change?

Figure 9-3

Take the time to review what worked and what could have been improved. When lessons learned are captured and incorporated into the next initiative, organizations are able to start at a higher, more-experienced level. The methodologies your people developed and the records of their actions can make it far easier for you and the organization as a whole to accelerate the next change initiatives.

Key Takeaways from Chapter 9

1. Leaders can use measurements to lead, assess, and maintain the change initiation, in terms of both the business plan and the leader change roadmap.

2. Leaders must understand what needs to be measured and focus on that.

3. Leaders must build a culture of measurement, so that everyone in the organization understands how progress will be assessed. The steps in building this culture include: setting and communicating realistic targets, building a set of metrics to keep everyone focused on results, using metrics to shape adoption and action, creating transparency, identifying small wins along the way, failing fast, and capturing lessons learned.

Chapter 10

Keep People Engaged, Accountable, and Productive

They say that time changes things, but you actually change them yourself.

—*Andy Warhol*

You, as leader, are accountable for creating the environment that enables change. You own the vision that gives people the reason to believe. You decide how to frame the messages that offer people a compelling reason to want to be part of the solution. You provide the resources that help people carry out the work. You facilitate and guide the team to find the most effective and reliable paths to implement solutions that lead to the results you defined. You know that, when you can ignite higher performance, results come more quickly and more efficiently and can be sustained over time. Your job is to get your people engaged and producing results. As you engage leaders at all levels to cascade timely, consistent, motivating messages and behaviors, the change becomes real. Until your people start working in the new way, the change initiative remains merely an interesting concept. By consistently reinforcing the new way, your people move from acceptance to action.

Three Aspects of Change Execution

There are three aspects to the execution of a change effort: engagement, accountability, and productivity. Each of these aspects enables the others.

- **Engagement** – People get involved and take action.
- **Accountability** – People feel a sense of ownership for the work and the success of the project. They are personally committed to the outcome and are willing to make decisions and take the appropriate action to follow through on what needs to be done.
- **Productivity** – People are actively engaged, they are accountable for their work in the change effort, and their work is advancing the effort forward.

Can you have engagement without accountability? Does accountability drive engagement? Can you be productive if people aren't engaged and don't feel accountable?

As a leader, you determine the level of engagement, accountability, and productivity that is required for each situation. You determine what you need to do to propel others to action. Those businesses that have highly engaged people who feel accountable for their work, and are efficiently producing work, are able to attain and sustain results.

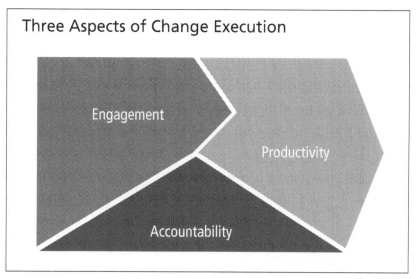

Figure 10-1

Engagement

Engagement is about accepting what's happening and doing something positive about the situation. People become engaged when they personally choose to get involved. They have made the decision to take action based on the information they have been given.

Leaders can help people choose to get engaged even after the energy from the announcement dies down and the true work in executing the change begins. Even if your people may have accepted the change, they often need reminders about the purpose and direction of the initiative. They may also need assistance in diagnosing problems and determining the right actions. To stay engaged, your people may need confirmation that their efforts are leading to the right results. Further, they may need motivation and inspiration, especially when the work takes longer or is more challenging than anticipated. This is why ongoing leadership involvement and communications are vital to keeping the change effort alive.

Stay Focused on Short-Term Goals

In times of uncertainty, staying focused on short-term goals keeps people focused on a key set of actions. As we've discussed in prior chapters, short-term goals enable short-term wins, which can be celebrated to keep the energy high and momentum active. Short-term goals give people both tangible measurements and a set of clear actions that they can influence.

Be Careful Not to Overmanage

When you cross over from coaching and supporting to doing their work, your people can start to feel micromanaged. There is a difference between observing/coaching and hovering/telling. Be clear about roles and expectations so that people are not confused over their roles and when and where you will be involved. Usually people get stuck for a reason. If work isn't being carried out as planned, figure out what may be missing to enable people to complete the tasks. Give your people the room to develop their actions from the business plan. Provide the scope of the work and get people involved in figuring out how to get the work done.

Give People Room to Act

When people feel that you will provide a safe environment to test ideas and solutions, they are more apt to try new approaches. This doesn't mean that you let people go off and do anything they want. It means you develop ideas, understand and mitigate the risks, and know when and how long to try a new approach. Throughout, you need to be as engaged as the team so that you can provide the support necessary to explore options.

The Power of Saying "No"

With so many activities going on, your people are likely buried in work. They may want to be engaged but struggle to find the time to do an adequate job at a new task. Since most have pride in their work, they may delay taking on new tasks, waiting for a block of time to get things organized and under way. Something has to give. Someone has to find the power to say "no" to make room for the new activities to emerge. Your people will be seeking your permission to let some actions go. Without the power of "no," people make trade-offs based on what's most pressing to them at the time; their decisions may not be aligned with what's best for your change initiative.

Create a Culture that Embraces Change

Help people get comfortable with change. It's here to stay. It's not personal, it's about growth and opportunity. Find ways to build resiliency into the work. Recognize where people are in adopting the change process, then provide the necessary support. Make it fun to get involved in something new. A change culture is a continuously learning culture.

Accountability

When people move from doing work to being accountable for the work, they are more likely to support the changes. Accountability is about what you expect from yourself and your people and what you – and they – are willing to do to execute the work. Being accountable means you and they are willing to adapt to the change.

Accountability is a broad set of behaviors. Accountability builds resiliency as people own what's happening to them and as they can accommodate the changes. They don't have to make all the decisions or have all the answers to be accountable. Sometimes decisions need to be made with only a few data points. It is critical that people are conscious of the situation and have made a decision to be actively involved in what happens, going forward.

In organizations where people feel accountable, they have a sense of ownership of their work. They feel valued for their expertise, and they recognize that they are part of something greater than themselves. Organizations that create accountability recognize and acknowledge both successes and failures and don't punish the failures. Accountable leaders will be able to make the adjustments to keep initiatives on track. Effectiveness improves when people have accountability for their work and the results they produce.

What Accountability Looks Like

- Assumes responsibility for making decisions, solving problems, and taking action
- Sets goals and takes responsibility for results
- Demonstrates a level of caring about the people and the situation; is committed to working with others on a viable solution
- Tackles any issues as they arise and figures out ways to make it work
- Accepts personal responsibility – proactively takes initiative; meets deadlines; keeps others informed; admits mistakes
- Works through adversities; removes obstacles and resolves conflicts
- Accepts responsibility for taking corrective action when solutions are off-target
- Helps and supports others
- Is committed to doing the right things
- Surfaces and tackles problems
- Seeks advice and input from others

Figure 10-2

Build a Culture of Accountability

Organizations that create a culture of ownership will typically create a safe environment for people to work. This starts with establishing transparent and clear communications, building trust, and respecting your people. It grows when you create forums for collaboration and encourage both thinking and problem-solving. It flourishes when you build a trusting environment where your

What a Lack of Accountability Looks Like

+ Blaming and finger pointing
+ Making excuses
+ Complaining
+ Creating drama
+ Procrastinating
+ Pouting
+ Playing the victim
+ Hoping for a miracle
+ Saying one thing and doing another
+ Second-guessing decisions and not supporting them

Figure 10-3

people can develop and grow. Under these conditions, accountability becomes everyone's responsibility.

People will be assessing how much control they actually have over what they do, when they accomplish it, and how they make decisions and carry out the work. They will want to know how much accountability they have and how much control they have in being accountable. When people have control over the what?, when?, and how? relative to their work, they become more engaged, take ownership, and are more productive.

So how can you get people to be more accountable for the change effort?

+ Lead by example– be a role model of accountability.
+ Operate with honesty and integrity. Be clear about what is nonnegotiable, so that people are not surprised.

- Build trust by being straightforward, transparent, and thoughtful in how you communicate and engage people in change. Cultivate trust by acknowledging the work of others.
- Set mutual expectations and define the span of control so people know where decisions are made and how to work with one another.
- Define the scope of the accountability and agree on the desired outcomes.
- Share successes and own the failures.
- Give people choice – create a culture that cares what people think. Let people have a voice and input into the work product.
- Use the power of feedback to provide people the knowledge to enhance future actions.
- Smooth out the bumps and hiccups by offering resources and removing impediments.
- Work collaboratively, using goals, metrics, and plans.
- Make accountability a normal way of operating.

CASE IN POINT

Building Accountability through Behavior

Sales were lagging in one company. Senior management was accountable for all aspects of the business. No decisions were made without senior management approval. This caused huge bottlenecks and missed opportunities throughout the company. The new president implemented a growth strategy and a business team structure to push accountability lower in the organization.

Senior management delegated decision-making to the business teams. Those teams were accountable for creating the product strategy and running the business. While this was a welcome change, senior management realized that the business teams continued to push decisions up to them.

Senior management realized that it wasn't enough to talk about accountability. While they talked about that guiding principle, their behaviors hadn't changed. Senior management agreed to adopt the following behaviors to drive accountability down to the business teams:

◆ Give the business teams decision-making authority.

◆ Listen, observe, and ask teams for recommendations.

◆ Remove obstacles that inhibit the business teams from doing their jobs.

◆ Give plenty of positive feedback as the teams create high-performing behaviors.

◆ Create learning opportunities to share cross-organizational best practices.

◆ Celebrate the business teams' small wins and advances.

With this concerted effort, the business teams were operating in a new way within a month. By moving accountability to the business teams, the organization was able to accelerate market decisions, which spurred growth.

Productivity

Your people can be both engaged and accountable, but if they aren't actually productive, their energy and ownership will not guide the organization to the results. Productivity requires energy to drive the effort. With the massive amount of work that needs to be accomplished, people need a way to organize and simplify actions into smaller tasks that can be completed effectively and efficiently.

To be productive requires focus. That means turning off distractions like emails, cell phones, and the Internet. Productivity is about forward movement, which means that there is little or no room for complaining, gossiping, or creating rumors. Productivity is working on the task at hand and minimizing any disruptions.

CHANGE LEADERSHIP ACTIONS

- ◆ Keep people engaged by:
  - ■ Staying focused on short-term goals
  - ■ Not overmanaging
  - ■ Giving people room to act
  - ■ Giving people the power to say "no"
  - ■ Creating a culture that embraces change
- ◆ Give people a sense of ownership in the work, so that they accept accountability for the results.
- ◆ Organize the work so that your people can work productively.

Figure 10-4

That can be easier said than done. To be productive requires carving out time for the most important tasks. I am a proponent of breaking activities into 15- to 20-minute tasks, versus believing you will find an hour or more time slot on your calendar. If a given task is really important, as most tasks are during change initiatives, it should be the very first thing you work on.

When people are engaged, they own the outcome, and they have the ability to be productive, actions are accelerated, so results begin to take shape.

Key Takeaways from Chapter 10

1. People become engaged when they personally choose to get involved. Leaders can encourage engagement by staying focused on short-term goals, giving people room to perform, and creating a culture that embraces change.

2. People become accountable when they get a sense of ownership and responsibility. When people have accountability, they act productively; when they don't take accountability, they can fall into blaming others, making excuses, and acting counter-productively. Leaders can build a culture of accountability by creating a trusting environment and giving people a measure of control over their work.

3. People become productive when they put energy into their work. Leaders can encourage productivity by removing distractions, helping people focus on the crucial work, and creating a culture of accomplishment and achieving results.

Chapter 11

Accelerate the Change

The quicker you let go of old cheese, the sooner you find new cheese.

—*Spencer Johnson, in* Who Moved My Cheese?

The Five A's in the Leader Change Framework

By using the Leader Change Framework (introduced in Chapter 3), you can think through how you will engage your people, hold them accountable, and harness all of them to accelerate the change initiative and therefore achieve the results. Let's review the parts of this model:

1. Accountability

Your people must acknowledge that the change is necessary and be accountable for their work in the initiative. Organizations that engage their people and help people feel ownership for their work are able to be more productive in achieving the business outcomes. Building accountability is key to sustaining the change solution. You can facilitate this by staying informed and gaining the input about what is happening throughout the change process that will help you get the necessary work done.

2. Agreement & Alignment

You must work to get your leadership team to reach agreement about the change, about why the change is important, and about how success will be measured. Go beyond the strategy and create both a compelling case for change (Chapter 3) and a develop your leader change roadmap to guide the initiative (Chapter 4). When they have clarity about the change, your leadership team and your people will be able to align themselves with the actions needed to implement the plan.

3. Acceptance

Change will test people physically, mentally, and emotionally. You must work to help your people understand and accept the need for change as quickly as possible, so that they can become active in the change initiative (Chapter 7). While we can't change people, we *can* show them the opportunity and direction to encourage them to work productively and focus on their parts in the overall initiative.

4. Action

Your actions, as change leader, should demonstrate how you want your people to behave. Be consistent and persistent in facilitating the change, so that new behaviors will emerge. The concepts in Chapter 1 can help you prepare to lead change. Use the change leadership behaviors (outlined in Chapter 4) to fast-track the change process and reinforce the new way.

Satisfying Individual Needs Increases Action. As people are assessing the change, they are looking to see how the change affects their work and needs. As leader, if you can help your people see what the change means to them and how it satisfies their needs, you will be better positioned to get your people to choose to be involved. Your people will ask questions like the following:

1. **"What can I expect?"** People want certainty and a level of control over what happens to them. Be transparent. Don't leave them hanging, only to think the worst. Let people know what's going to happen to them. Help them see the opportunity and make choices.

2. **"How will you spark my interest?"** People like variety and different experiences even when they hang onto the status quo. They want new experiences, and at the same time they want control and certainty that they won't be put into any adverse situations.

3. **"Is it worth it?"** People want to know that what they are doing has value as well as significance.

4. **"How does this provide me with connection?"** People like to be part of a community. Organizations provide them with a social aspect to their work. If there is a change, people want to know that they will have connections to others.

5. **"How does this help me with my own personal growth?"** People want to know how your initiative can help them grow and develop, both professionally and personally.

6. **"How does my work contribute to something larger than me?"** People want to get a sense that they are contributing to large goals, to something that has meaning over the long term.

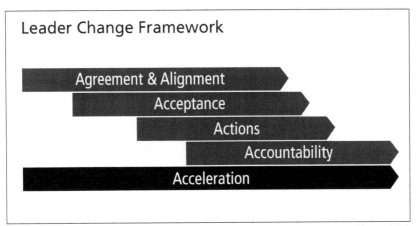

Figure 11-1

The Role of the Leader in the 5th A: Acceleration

Continue Building Your Change Culture

Don't ignore the culture shifts that occur with change. Many leaders are afraid to address the culture, but remember that whenever you ask people to work in a new way, you are adjusting the culture of the organization. Culture is the pattern of behaviors – what people are doing and saying, and the ways of working. When a new initiative is introduced, we can assume that people will work in the same ways, until they are moved to work in new ways. Your people need to see that the familiar patterns of behavior will not allow the organization to move to the new ways of working that yield new results. If you want to motivate others, look for things that will immediately reinforce the new behaviors.

Motivate Your People

You need to know what motivates your people, as a group and individually. Motivations may vary somewhat from person to person – some people are focused on money, while others want professional satisfaction, and so forth – but you can make some general assumptions about what will make your people want to put their best efforts into the change initiative. For most people, a prime motivator is being truly involved in the work. You can involve them by giving them the information they need to be productive and acknowledging their accomplishments.

Accelerate Results through Ongoing Reinforcement

What you do and say as a leader has a huge impact on the success or failure of the change effort. Leading change isn't a process that you can glide through or opt out of when certain aspects don't appeal to you. If you want results and want to accelerate the change, you must focus deeply on the people side of the implementation.

Often, you need to modify your behavior first. Accelerating change takes an awareness and observation to assess whether your actions are helping or hindering the actions of others. You need to create the environment, provide the resources, and ignite the spark so that others will want to take action. The environment must enable your people to get going – and keep on going. You have done your work in creating the environment if you:

- Help people understand the idea and the goals underlying the change initiative.
- Outline a clear path forward.
- Create conditions to prepare people for the change.
- Inspire and motivate your people to see the value in the change.
- Remove the obstacles and resolve the issues that might have interfered with getting the work done.

You can take specific actions to accelerate the change:

- Make sure your communications are clear and that they provide the information your people need to take action.
- Establish high standards of excellence and be willing to coach and mentor people to reach these standards.
- Reinforce productive behaviors by giving people the feedback that tells them they are moving in the right direction.

Too many leaders say this work is far too hard. But if you want the results, you need to do it. Do you want to accelerate the change? Then identify the undesirable behaviors. Find out what's enabling these undesirable behaviors to occur, and provide immediate feedback to redirect actions to a desirable behavior. As soon as people start exhibiting the desired behaviors, provide positive feedback to motivate additional actions.

CHANGE LEADERSHIP ACTIONS
♦ Use the Leader Change Framework to drive implementation of your change initiative.
♦ Focus on the "Acceleration" part of the model by:
■ Continuing to build your change culture
■ Motivating your people
■ Accelerating results through ongoing reinforcement, coaching, and staff development
■ Creating a mentality of abundance, not scarcity

Figure 11-2

If you go to **www.thetruthaboutchangebook.com** and click on "Free Book Bonuses," you will find a downloadable copy of the Leader Change Framework: The Five Keys to Leading Change.

Create a Mentality of Abundance, not Scarcity

Studies show that a scarcity model works well in some cases by enticing people to purchase goods and services or getting them to take short-term actions to accommodate the scarcity. Just like the carrot-and-stick approach, the scarcity mentality can quickly become unproductive. If you use the scarcity approach too often, people stop listening. People do not tire from abundance. Abundance and opportunity breed more opportunity. If you want your people to become more engaged in productive actions, create conditions that reinforce and encourage the new way.

Key Takeaways from Chapter 11

1. The Leader Change Framework – Accountability, Agreement & Alignment, Acceptance, Action, and Acceleration – promotes actions that keep the organization moving through change implementation toward results.

2. People accelerate their actions when they see how the change benefits them.

3. Leaders can accelerate change toward goals by: building a change culture; motivating the people; reinforcing change through coaching and staff development; and creating a sense of abundance, not scarcity.

Final Thoughts:
Letter to a Change Leader

Things do not change; we change.

—*Henry David Thoreau*

Dear Jack:

I couldn't be happier with the progress you have made with your department. You and your team have created a well-thought-out business plan to position your organization as a marketplace leader.

Over the course of your career, you have experienced a lot of change, large and small, and have led many change initiatives. You have developed your own set of tools to implement organizational changes. As we've discussed, paying attention to strategy, processes, and plans is not enough to ensure results. Successful change initiatives need leaders and people ready, willing, and able to make the changes. Before you and your team get started on deploying the business plan, I want to review some ideas that our organization has found helpful in successfully executing key initiatives.

Let's go over some truths about change. These truths remind us that implementation requires highly engaged and motivated people to bring initiatives to life. Some of these truths are obvious, but can be overlooked or discounted, if you forget that the changes require a journey to move people from the present to the future.

1. While leaders may have strong technical skills and business acumen, they may not know how to lead – or are not comfortable leading – others through change. Change starts when you become personally accountable for the initiative and are willing to address all aspects that can affect how people become engaged and committed to making the business changes. I would like to see you develop a leader change roadmap to integrate the business plan and a project implementation plan with the appropriate leadership and stakeholder plans to ensure that the people aspects are addressed and that you and your team can accelerate the change.

2. Solving business problems usually involves making changes. If you want new results, you need to move your people into a new way of acting and behaving. Your business plan alone will not engage your people; you need a case for change along with clear communications to gain their acceptance and alignment.

3. Your time is taken up with planning strategies and tactics, so the people aspects of the initiative tend to get shortchanged. You can accelerate the change and build accountability throughout your organization by spending equal or more time ensuring that your people are ready and able to achieve the desired results.

4. People want the benefits of change, but do not want to actually *be* changed. To achieve results, you need to gain buy-in, which starts with people seeing "what's in it for them" or how they can be of service. If you simply tell people to "just do it," you won't get either the actions or the behaviors you need. Your plans should identify the specific behaviors and the positive reinforcement you will use to accelerate action.

5. Change is disruptive and can trigger fears of failure. Fear can minimize actions, which in turn can compromise results. You need to assess how the change will affect your people and how difficult it will be for them to adopt new behaviors. Then, you need to help your people address the physical, emotional, mental, and spiritual challenges, so that they will quickly move to a new way of working.

6. Initiatives fall apart in implementation when an organization lacks agreement and alignment. Setting a clear direction gives your people a clear roadmap to follow.

7. People will naturally do the activities they enjoy and avoid ones that are uncomfortable or difficult. You need to provide ample positive reinforcement through coaching and feedback to encourage your people to perform the new actions. This will accelerate the change initiative.

You can't ignore the truth that people play a critical role in making the change happen and delivering the new results. Implementing the change won't always be comfortable for you and your team. You and your people have to learn new skills and incorporate different approaches at a time when you are already under tremendous pressure to deliver what's currently on your plate. To achieve sustainable business results, you need to help others *want* to make changes. It's not enough to get people to comply, as the results will not be sustainable over time.

In every change initiative, you need to determine how you and other leaders need to be involved to help people move to the new way of working. When you are serious about actually leading change (not just managing it), you can inspire your people to take the journey to a new, more productive way of working.

Remember the five key elements of the Leader Change Framework. As you think through each element, you can gain many insights about what you need to do to engage your people.

Agreement & Alignment

- How are you engaging your leadership team in agreeing to and aligning with the business change?
- Is there agreement and alignment by the leadership team?
- Do people understand the case for change – the what, why, how?
- What are your plans to socialize the change initiative throughout the organization?

Awareness, Acceptance, and Engagement

◆ Who is affected by the change?

◆ What do you need them to do?

◆ How will they react to the change?

◆ How can you help people acknowledge, accept, and engage in the work?

Adoption and Action

◆ Do you have a leader change roadmap that aligns implementation activities with leader and individual performer actions?

◆ Are the new behaviors and consequence systems clearly aimed at cascading these behaviors through your organization? What information, training, and support do people need to get started?

◆ Do any cross-organizational interdependencies need to be addressed?

◆ How will you get your people quickly working in the new way?

Acceleration

◆ How can you use feedback, coaching, and other positive consequences to accelerate the change?

◆ How can you celebrate the small wins that add up to big results?

Accountability and Progress

◆ How will you track progress?

◆ Are people able to perform the new work without being prompted?

◆ What can you do to help people take ownership for working in the new way?

◆ How are you incorporating lessons learned into your next initiative?

The change tools and methodologies we've discussed can be used for all business changes, large and small. When you have practiced several times what you've learned, the change leadership methodologies will become part of your personal leadership toolkit. You will find yourself naturally doing the work in both the business plan *and* the leader change roadmap.

I know you want to accelerate the change process to get results quickly. The more you want to accelerate, the more important it is to pay attention to the people side of change. You need to have the conversations, communicate with your people, and do the work, so that you and your people can execute the changes simply and cleanly. Change leadership enables implementation and must be woven into all your business actions and initiatives.

Jack, thank you for attending to the people side of change with as much energy and enthusiasm as you and your team have done. Thank you for being willing to act as a change-savvy leader and help your people go beyond what they thought was possible. With your steady and capable leadership, I know that you and your organization will easily meet or exceed the business plan targets.

Here's to bringing your best to leading change,
Hilary Potts

Dream it. Plan it. Lead it. Be it. Achieve it.

Acknowledgments

Like leading change, writing a book happens through the active support of numerous people who have the passion and the desire to take a concept and use it to create a solution that can help many.

Countless people have served roles to bring this book into your hands – some are noted here, but many are from my client engagements or even brief encounters. These are people I meet in my travels who are willing to share their stories and experiences with both successful and failed changes. You are what I call the true "book angels," a concept I learned when my son Evan hiked the Appalachian Trail. Along the way he would encounter people, "trail angels," who provided random acts of kindness that helped him on his journey.

In my journey to write this book, I have been fortunate to have many of my own "book angels" who shared their stories and experiences, who shared their truth about change, who provided support, a friendly suggestion, or even a quiet place to write. For those who have been on this journey with me, you hold a close place in my heart. Thank you.

I am grateful for the leaders I have been fortunate to work with and who have influenced and shaped me over the decades – leaders who have shown me the many approaches to leading change, some more effective than others. And the Great Women Group who in the early stages of the book provided insights and ideas on what they saw as the difference between a change, a transition, and a transformation. We had some marvelous exchanges and came to the realization that our definitions were different based on our role, experience, and situation, with the constant that the truth about change elicits physical, mental, emotional, and even spiritual reactions.

I appreciate the help and support of many colleagues, clients, and friends – you know who you are, and I thank you for your thoughtfulness and willingness to listen and provide your opinions. A special note of thanks to my dear friend Dr. Bhagwati Mistry, who, whenever I would call to take a break or go on an excursion, she never hesitated, never asked; she just held the sacred space that I needed in that moment.

As with my first book, a team of people helped to birth this book. A debt of gratitude and huge thanks to Deirdre Silberstein, who has been with me from the start and took this project on as her own. She is a talented, accomplished strategic editor and business consultant who is well versed in business and has the ability to simplify and pare down information into succinct concepts. I am grateful for her wisdom and advice as well as her ability to help me bring my own authentic voice to the page.

I am grateful to Lynn Amos for her creativity to take words and create visual pictures of the concepts. I am thrilled with her clean and simple interior layout, her creative illustrations, and her book cover design.

Thank you, Mark Woodworth, whom I was thrilled to work with again on the copy editing and proofing of this book. He makes the process easy and fun, bringing the book from a manuscript to the final product.

To my accountability partners, Jasbindar Singh and Stuart Elliot, my sounding board, who never tired of my weekly discussions and were willing partners in reviewing early drafts and have been a sounding board from start to finish. Thank you, Christy Tryhus and John Eggen at Mission Publishing, who have taught me the process of writing and publishing a book. Christy's coaching and enormous positive energy and encouragement helped me keep things going among the many distractions. I appreciate the support of Tom Buford, whose behind-the-scenes support of messaging was most helpful. A special thanks to Graham Van Dixhorn for devising the subtitle and creating cover copy.

The manuscript benefited from the thoughtful review by a dear colleague, Frits Vranken. It was fun to collaborate on early drafts and I appreciate his frank and invaluable advice to tell the truth that leading change isn't always fun or for the faint of heart. Thanks to Elaine Caprio for her early review of the book and her creative ideas to ensure that a variety of readers can pick up ideas and key takeaways to implement in their organization.

To the next generation and my children, Garrett and Evan, I am so proud of you and what you have become, each following your passion to make a positive contribution to the world. I learn from you and your friends as you navigate through the many changes life brings your way. You are open, inquisitive, and willing to show me different perspectives of the world. To Garrett's lovely partner, Kellie: I value our conversations and your many questions about why leaders do what they do and how to navigate today's business environment.

Thank you to the love of my life, my darling husband and life partner, Michael House, who keeps me grounded in reality and never lets my feet get too far off the ground. I'm grateful to you for all the hours you spent listening to my banter and helping me bring this book to the world. Without your support, it would not have been written.

May this book bring all who take the time to read it some new and inspired approaches to leading change. For those already expert at change, may it be a reminder that while you may have been down this path before, your colleagues may be reacting and experiencing the change very differently than you. Here's to bringing your best self to leading yourself and others.

About the Author

Hilary Potts, founder of The HAP Group, serves as an advisor and coach to some of the world's most prominent organizations as they manage delicate, complex situations and map out strategies to turn challenges into viable business solutions. Hilary has dedicated her career to helping others perform at their best while leading strategic business change. Her work is built on a strong foundation of practical business experience, extensive consulting expertise, and deep transformational practices.

With over three decades of experience in leading and advising organizations, Hilary knows firsthand the importance of creating and implementing strategies to develop leaders and grow healthy companies. She served as CEO and President for a global leader in performance-based consulting. She spent the first fifteen years of her career at a Fortune 500 chemical company, where she held a variety of sales and business management positions.

Drawing on her expertise, Hilary has written *The Executive Transition Playbook: Strategies for Starting Strong, Staying Focused, and Succeeding in Your New Leadership Role.* The book offers senior leaders powerful principles and practices for achieving a smarter, smoother transition during a leader's first days and weeks in a new role.

Hilary lives in Middlebury, Connecticut. She enjoys spending time with her husband, Michael House, and two sons, Garrett and Evan, cycling, golfing, hiking, and enjoying whatever life brings her way.

To communicate with Hilary Potts about her availability for speaking engagements or working with you and your organization, visit her website: www.HilaryPotts.com.

Resources to Help You Lead Change

Now that you have read *The Truth About Change*, you have additional knowledge and insights about how to guide yourself and others through challenging business times. So often, we are introduced to new concepts, but do not apply them. My hope is that you have been inspired to action and will use this leader change framework to help navigate a current strategic business initiative. Achieving successful change and new results requires people doing things differently. To help you see real and lasting results, I strongly recommend that you take advantage of the resources below within the next 24 hours:

www.thetruthaboutchangebook.com

- ◆ The Truth About Change Readiness Questionnaire
- ◆ Leader Change Framework: The 5 Keys to Leading Change
- ◆ Five Change Leadership Behaviors to Add to Your Daily Routine

A full range of resources for organizational and personal leadership are available including free downloads, articles, podcasts, and Hilary's blog.

Hilary and The HAP Group team are devoted to advising individuals and organizations on effectively navigating change. For more details on how you can book Hilary and her team for speaking events, consulting and coaching engagements, or workshop programs, send an email to hilarypotts@hapgrp.com.

Follow Hilary on Twitter: www.twitter.com/Hilary_Potts
Visit Facebook: www.Facebook.com/HAPGroup1

Spreading the Word

Leading change can be difficult, lonely, and overwhelming work without the right level of support from colleagues and others. At The HAP Group, we don't believe it needs to be this way, and we're looking to you to help spread the word. Who do you know that is navigating a strategic initiative? If you have been inspired by the content in *The Truth About Change* and want to support others in successfully leading change, here are some action steps you can take to make a difference:

- ◆ Give *The Truth About Change* to colleagues, friends, family members, and anyone you think could use support in being part of a change effort. This will make the journey to the new way less lonely and more engaging for them.

- ◆ Share your thoughts about *The Truth About Change* on Twitter, Facebook, LinkedIn, and other sites where people who lead change go for information, ideas, support, and sometimes just a boost. Feel free to write a blog post or a book review to help others successfully lead change.

- ◆ Collaborate with others on this approach to engaging others in a change effort. Purchase copies of the book for your team so that you can use a consistent change leadership framework.

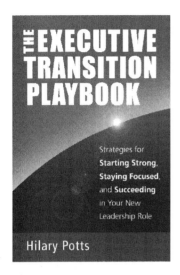

Don't just survive your leader transition. *Thrive* in it!

You are expected to get up to speed and add value to the business. *Fast.*

Hilary Potts offers powerful principles and practices to achieve a smarter, smoother transition. You will learn what to do and think about at each step, and will establish the platform for success well beyond your transition.

◆ Create a step-by-step plan to accelerate your learning and momentum.

◆ Know the classic transition mistakes and learn how to avoid them.

◆ Open communication channels and build trusting relationships across all levels.

◆ See even the subtlest warning signs that your transition is off track.

◆ Make clear, conscious choices about how you want to lead.

"Moving into a new role is a big challenge for any leader at any level. Read this book and let executive coach Hilary Potts help to make your leadership transition a smooth and successful one."

Ken Blanchard, coauthor of *The New One Minute Manager* and *Collaboration Begins with You*

Visit **www.executivetransitionplaybook.com** *to download the first two chapters of The Executive Transition Playbook.*

ISBN 978-1-51536-075-9 (paperback) US $19.95
Kindle, ASIN: B015QBK5BG US $9.99
Available on Amazon.com & Barnesandnoble.com

Made in the USA
Middletown, DE
03 October 2017